Advanced Pragmatic Psychology

SUSANNA MITTERMAIER

GARY M. DOUGLAS

Advanced Pragmatic Psychology
Copyright © 2020 by Gary M. Douglas & Susanna Mittermaier
ISBN: 978-1-63493-369-8

All rights reserved. No part of this publication may be reproduced, stored in a retrieval system, or transmitted, in any form or by any means electronic, mechanical, photocopying, recording, or otherwise without prior written permission from the publisher.

The author and publisher of the book do not make any claim or guarantee for any physical, mental, emotional, spiritual, or financial result. All products, services and information provided by the author are for general education and entertainment purposes only. The information provided herein is in no way a substitute for medical advice. In the event you use any of the information contained in this book for yourself, the author and publisher assume no responsibility for your actions.

Published by Access Consciousness® Publishing

Advanced Pragmatic Psychology

Creating a Life on Planet Earth
Without Trauma or Drama,
Upset or Intrigue

GARY M. DOUGLAS

SUSANNA MITTERMAIER

ACCESS CONSCIOUSNESS PUBLISHING

TABLE OF CONTENTS

Introduction..1

The Access Consciousness Clearing Statement®.................3

Chapter 1: What Is Pragmatic Psychology?.....................7
  What are We Creating by the Choices We are Making?
  Getting Pragmatic About What is Going On
  Changing This Reality

Chapter 2: Knowing Is The Ultimate Resource.................12

**Chapter 3: A Different Possibility Is Available
With Allowance**..15
  Allowance vs. the Need to Be Right
  Tool: Interesting Point of View I Have This Point of View
  The Space of Allowance
  Clearing: Living From, As, and With Awareness and Knowing

Chapter 4: The Joy of Judgment or The Joy of Awareness......19
  The Joy that Awareness Gives You
  Conclusions, Results, Answers, and Completions
  Eliminating All Conclusions
  Moving Beyond Interpretation
  Interpretation Keeps You from Being Present with What Is
  Clearing: Interpreting Energies that Cannot be Translated

Chapter 5: The Extreme Sport Of Awareness...................26
  What if You Could Enjoy Being Totally Present in Each Moment?
  An Intense Level of Receiving
  The Ability to Choose More

Chapter 6: Choosing More..................................31
    Choose and See What Happens
    Being Pragmatic is Embracing All Choices

Chapter 7: Would You Like To Have More Money?..............35
    Start Paying You 10 Percent Before You Pay for Anything Else
    "Wow! I Have Money!"
    The Space of Money
    Using Money to Create a Future
    Make a Demand

Chapter 8: The Ease And Joy Of Living......................42
    The Planet is Hedonistic and Abundant Beyond Belief
    What Would You Do if Your Life was Total Ease?
    Can You Have Everything You Desire?
    The Sense of Wanting or Lacking
    Want Is Not a Real Word
    What Haven't You Acknowledged that You're Actually Capable Of?
    Celebrate Creation
    Creating the Judgment of Wealth
    There's Nothing Wrong with Being Judged
    Playing Creates Much More Money than Work Does
    Clearing: Become a Playmate of Consciousness
    Life as Play
    Clearing: Become an Orchestrator of Consciousness
    Never Enough but Always Too Much to Spend

Chapter 9: Putting The Productive Elements of Life Into Motion...57
    Producing vs. Doing
    Create a More Productive Reality

Chapter 10: Pragmatic Relationships........................61
    Trying to Fit Yourself Into the Relationship Box
    A Relationship That Truly Works for You
    Tool: Does This Work for Me?

What About Getting Pragmatic in Your Relationship?
Trying to Make Someone Happy
Your Awareness Creates a Place Where You are Never Alone

Chapter 11: Pragmatic Parenting..................................68
What if What You Choose as a Parent is Not Wrong?
Truth, Lies, and Secrets
The Biggest Gift is the Truth
Secrets Solidify Your Awareness
Quality Time
Ask Your Kids Questions
Questions Enable You to Find Out What is Going On
Child Rearing
Give Up Control
Family
What Have You Decided Family Is?
Do You Have a Responsibility to Your Family?
Clearing: How Much of Your Awareness Are You Stultifying With The Family You are Holding Onto for Dear Life?

Chapter 12: Working With People In A Pragmatic Way..........79
What Works is Different for Each Person
Change Comes from Allowance, Not from a Point of View
How Can You Change Someone's Point of View?
True Caring
What Seeds are You Planting Right Now?
Moving Beyond the Conversation and Cognitizing of Mainstream Psychology
Information and Tools You Can Use in Working with Yourself and Others
Generosity of Spirit vs. Envy and Jealousy

Chapter 13: Marketing Yourself: Creating The Package.........96
  Be Interested in Everyone
  Choose Elegance
  Ask: How Can I Use This Package to My Advantage?
  Go to Social Events

Chapter 14: The Point Where All Things Become Possible....102
  Clearing: What Have You Made So Vital About Never Being Totally Relaxed?
  Are You Avoiding the Complexity and the Joy of Choosing Possibility?
  Becoming a Being Who Can Create Worlds and Possibilities
  Clearing: Receiving the Title Omnipotent Infinite Being
  You Don't Have to Fight Against This Reality to Create a New Reality
  Creating from the Exquisite Moments of Being
  What Comes to You is the Result of Choices You Make
  The Gentleness of All Possibility

Chapter 15: Questions And Tools You Can Use To Open The Doors Of Possibilty...109
  Tool: What Else is Possible?
  Instead of Judging, Use "What Else Is Possible?"
  Tool: How Does it Get Any Better than This?
  Tool: Indulge the Thought
  Tool: Acknowledge What Is
  Tool: What Would I Have to Be or Do Differently that Would Create a Different Possibility Here?
  What If You Acknowledge What is True for You in Every Moment?
  Tool: What Awareness Can I Have Here that Would Erase All of This?
  Tool: What's Relevant Here?
  Never Give Up, Never Give In, Never Quit

INTRODUCTION

This book is based on a class facilitated by Gary Douglas and Susanna Mittermaier.

Susanna is a psychologist educated at the University of Lund in Sweden. She worked in child oncology and later in mental health, where she met patients with many different diagnoses. She has also done psychotherapy, neuropsychological testing, and staff counseling. Early in her career she began to search for something that could work even better than traditional psychology, and she came in contact with Access Consciousness, a worldwide movement with pragmatic tools that change thousands of lives every day.

Susanna met Gary Douglas, the founder of Access Consciousness, and after many conversations about what else could be possible with psychology, she founded Pragmatic Psychology.

Gary and Susanna invite you to turn what you have decided is a wrongness about you into the strongness you can be.

INTRODUCTION

What can we find, what can we know,
that we can institute and change the world
to a place that works better?

THE ACCESS CONSCIOUSNESS CLEARING STATEMENT®

You are the only one who can unlock the points of view that have you trapped.

The clearing process is a tool you can use to change the energy of the points of view that have you locked into unchanging situations.

Throughout this book, we ask a lot of questions. Some of those questions might twist your head around a little bit. That's our intention. The questions we ask are designed to get your mind out of its regular mode so you can get to the *energy* of a situation.

Once the question has twisted your head around and brought up the energy of a situation, we ask if you are willing to destroy and uncreate that energy—because stuck energy is the source of barriers and limitations. Destroying and uncreating that energy will open the door to new possibilities for you.

This is your opportunity to say, "Yes, I'm willing to let go of whatever is holding that limitation in place."

That opportunity is followed by some odd language that we call the clearing statement:

Right and Wrong, Good and Bad, POD and POC, All 9, Shorts, Boys, and Beyonds.

With the clearing statement, we're going back to the energy of the limitations and barriers that have been created. We're looking at the energies that keep us from moving forward and expanding into all the spaces we would like to go. The clearing statement addresses the energies that are creating the limitations and contractions in our lives.

The more you run the clearing statement, the deeper it goes and the more layers and levels it can unlock for you. If a lot of energy comes up for you in response to a question, you may wish to repeat the clearing process numerous times until the subject being addressed is no longer an issue for you.

Because it's about the energy, you don't have to understand the words of the clearing statement for it to work. However, if you're interested in knowing what the words mean, here are some brief definitions:

Right and Wrong, Good and Bad is shorthand for, "What's right, good, perfect, and correct about this? What's wrong, mean, vicious, terrible, bad, and awful about this?" The short version of these questions is, "What's right and wrong, good and bad?" This refers to the things we consider right, good, perfect, and/or correct that stick us the most. We have decided that we have them right, so we do not wish to let go of them.

POD stands for the **P**oint **o**f **D**estruction: all the ways you have been destroying yourself in order to keep whatever you're clearing in existence.

POC stands for the **P**oint **o**f **C**reation: all the thoughts, feelings, and emotions immediately preceding your decision to lock the energy in place.

When you "POD and POC" something, it is like pulling the bottom card out of a house of cards. The whole thing falls down. Some people say "POD and POC it" as shorthand for the entire statement.

All 9 stands for the nine different ways you have created this item as a limitation in your life. They are the layers of thoughts, feelings, emotions, and points of view that create the limitation as solid and real.

Shorts is the short version of a much longer series of questions. These include, "What's meaningful about this? What's meaningless about this? What's the punishment for this? What's the reward for this?"

Boys stands for energetic structures called nucleated spheres. These have to do with those areas of our lives where we've tried to handle something continuously with no effect. There are at least thirteen different kinds of these spheres, which are collectively called "the boys." A nucleated sphere looks like the bubbles created when you blow into a bubble pipe that has multiple chambers. It creates a huge mass of bubbles, and when you pop one bubble, the other bubbles fill in the space.

When you want to get to the core of an issue, have you ever tried to peel away the layers of the onion but could never get there? That's because it wasn't an onion; it was a nucleated sphere.

Beyonds are feelings or sensations that stop your heart and your willingness to look at possibilities. Beyonds are what occur when you are in shock. We have lots of areas in our lives where we freeze up. Anytime you freeze up, it's a beyond holding you captive. That's the difficulty with a beyond: It stops you from being present. The beyonds include everything that is beyond belief, reality, imagination, conception, perception, rationalization, and forgiveness. There are many other beyonds as well. They are usually feelings and sensations — rarely emotions and never thoughts.

You can choose to use the clearing statement or not. We don't have a point of view about that, but we invite you to try it and see what happens.

1

WHAT IS PRAGMATIC PSYCHOLOGY?

Psychology used to be the study of knowing. It turned into the study of behavior and what is sane or insane, good or bad, right or wrong.

Pragmatic Psychology is about doing what works and empowering you to choose that which creates the life and planet you desire. Rather than being dramatic, rather than looking at what does not work and why, pragmatic psychology invites you to turn on the lights so you can see what *is*—and find out what choices you have that will create the future you want. This is about looking at the way things are in the world and seeing them from a different point of view. It's about being in communication with everything and trusting what you know and what you are aware of. It's also about knowing how to ask questions and choosing to do what works. When you do these things, you see how to create a different future for yourself and the planet.

The state of our planet is a concern for us all. In Santa Barbara, where Gary lived for over forty years, the oak trees and the vegetation on the mountains are dying. The land is becoming more and more barren. Parts of it look like Lake Havasu, Arizona, a barren place where there is no shade nothing grows higher than your knees; it looks like a nuclear winter hit. This is currently being created in California. In forty years, Gary never saw Santa Barbara look the way it does today.

NASA has said that about a year's worth of underground water is left in California. There's a lot of land there and a lot of people. How is that going to work for the future? They are running out of water, yet in Santa Barbara we saw four housing projects under construction. Each development had at least forty houses. That's crazy.

History gives us many examples of this kind of craziness — where we haven't looked at the way things are in the world and how that's going to work in the future. Thousands of years ago, when the Romans went to Morocco and North Africa, there was an abundance of water. Forests covered the mountains. The Romans started moving the water from the mountains to the coast for their cities, and gradually the forests disappeared. There are now no more forests in that area of the world. It has been a desert for thousands of years.

What are We Creating by the Choices We are Making?

We have to ask, "What are we creating by the choices we are making?" We have to ask that because it gives us a sense of the future we are creating. When we simply align and agree with a point of view without looking at what it creates, we start to accept that point of view as our reality. We create that reality within the microcosm of our personal life and the macrocosm of the planet.

The wars in the Middle East are an example of aligning and agreeing with a point of view without looking at what it creates. Alignment and agreement about violence creates that violence as a reality. Israelis and Palestinians have been fighting on and off for over a hundred years. They have been fighting for so long that people don't even know why they're fighting anymore. It's just, "We don't like those guys," so they attack one another and perpetuate the violence they have aligned and agreed with. There is a complete absence of question and an unwillingness to see the future they are creating.

Getting Pragmatic About What is Going On

Most of us do a version of this in our own lives. The same topics, the same conflicts, the same issues keep coming up for us, and they stop us from creating what we truly desire in our life. We create all kinds of trauma and drama, upset and intrigue, and we make the agreements of this reality more vital and real than our knowing that things could be otherwise. We never get pragmatic about what's going on. We don't look at *what's actually going to work* or *what's actually going to create what we desire*. We just keep struggling with the same old things and are never able to create the life we want. We're stultified by this reality.

Stultification means stale and not changing, and it has a seductive way of creeping into our lives. Stultification seems comfortable and attractive to people who don't want things to change. They are content trying to fit themselves into a box, so they stultify themselves by taking points of view.

They say, "This is my place in the world. This is where I belong. This is my niche." They don't see the possibilities that are available to them; they simply swing back and forth within the narrowest range they can without ever asking a question or doing something different. They think their small, stultified reality *is* reality. But it is *not* reality. It is just a *point of view*. They stultify expansion so they don't lose their place, but, in the process, they create this reality as sludge—slow and stultified.

Changing This Reality

Fortunately, there are some beings on planet Earth who search and invent other possibilities. Out of a lack of satisfaction with the status quo, they create change. We call them *humanoids*. Humanoids are willing to be different. They have a target of creating the life they desire. They make a demand of themselves: "No matter what, I am having the life I desire as my reality!"

Many humanoids take this demand a step further and swear to themselves that no matter what it takes, they are going to change this reality. They say, "I am going to change this reality. I don't care what it takes. I don't care what it looks like. I don't care what I lose or gain in the process. None of that matters. What matters is the change that is possible."

Access Consciousness offers something that can create possibilities far beyond what mainstream psychology or psychotherapy can create. We ask, "What can we find, what can we know, that we can institute that will change the world into a place that works better?"

*We have to ask,
"What are we creating by the choices we are making?"
We have to look at that because it will give us
a sense of the future we are creating.*

KNOWING IS THE ULTIMATE RESOURCE

We'd like to give you the awareness of how you can begin to choose differently in your life. Knowing is the ultimate resource for beginning to choose something different. When you acknowledge your knowing, everything becomes available to you. All choices become available. And when you acknowledge *when* you know and *what* you know, the speed of your knowing increases dynamically.

When you start to function from knowing, the future becomes more obvious to you. You think, "I'm going to choose this." Then you ask, "How is that going to work?" You start to see that every choice you make creates a new future available to you.

For instance, Gary and Dr. Dain Heer, the co-creator of Access, were thinking about buying a castle in Milan, Italy, and they went to have a look at it. Once they got there, the future that was available with the castle became obvious to them. It was simply a matter of asking, "How is this going to work?" It was much too close to the brink of falling apart, so the obvious response was, "Okay, cool. Thank you for the information."

When you know that you know, you are aware of what's going on in the world around you. You don't align and agree, or resist and react, to what is happening. You simply say, "Oh, okay. Thank you." You receive what is going on as the gift of awareness. You ask,

- What do I know?
- What would I like to choose?

Then you ask, "What can I do with this?" You need to live *as that question*. If you're like most people, you receive the gift of awareness all the time — but don't ask what you can do about it. You say things like, "I don't like that. That doesn't feel good. I hate awareness because I can't do anything about it." No. You have to ask,

- What can I do with this?
- Do I want to change it?
- Can I change it?
- What can I change?

When Susanna founded Pragmatic Psychology, she did not have any information about what it would lead to or what it would look like. She just knew that it would create a future for many people and empower them to know that they know, rather than getting stuck in the difficulties of the past. Instead of looking for the false security of thinking and calculating, it was the lightness of knowing that guided her.

Once you can know what you know, things move a whole lot better. Life is lot more fun. You feel good about yourself. You have people lusting after you. Everybody looks at you and says, "Please, God, let me have what she has! Let me have what he has!"

When you know that you know,
you are aware of what's going on in the world around you.

You don't align and agree, or resist and react,
to what is happening.

You simply say, "Oh, okay. Thank you."

You receive what is going on as the gift of awareness.

3

A DIFFERENT POSSIBILITY IS AVAILABLE WITH ALLOWANCE

Once you know that you know and are aware of what's happening around you, you receive what is going on as the gift of awareness. This is called allowance, and it's a sublimely pragmatic way of being in the world.

Allowance is the attitude that everything is just an interesting point of view—no matter *what's* going on. It is a creative energy that allows you to be in the question and thus change anything. Allowance keeps the space of *you* available to you. From that space, you can know what you know and choose what works for you.

When you're in allowance, many things come at you—thoughts,

ideas, beliefs, attitudes, judgments, and emotions — but you're like a rock in the stream. Everything flows around you. You're still you. But if you start to resist and react, or align and agree, with those thoughts, ideas, beliefs, attitudes, judgments, or emotions, you are no longer aware. You are no longer the rock in the stream, and you get swept away in the current.

Instead of being in allowance, we often we try to do something with the things we are aware of. Let's say someone is rude to you by saying you are stupid and wrong. You might react. Or maybe a friend is planning to do something you think is colossally stupid. You might try to fix or handle them and, in the process, become the effect of them. But when you're in allowance, you are aware and nothing is required but a question: "Is this relevant?" If yes, then ask, "What is required here?"

Allowance vs. the Need to Be Right

Our need to be right — or our propensity to see ourselves as wrong — gets in the way of being in allowance. As soon as we adopt a point of view like "I'm so right!" or "I'm so wrong!" we come out of question and awareness and can no longer see clearly what's happening. For example, when somebody accuses you of something, you can go into agreement and say, "Maybe I really am as terrible as they say I am!" Or, you can resist and say, "Stupid person! How can they say this to me?" Both are forms of reaction, and neither gives you any freedom.

When you don't need to be right anymore, when your fallback position of always being wrong goes away, you can be in allowance — and life gets way easier.

- How much energy does it take to maintain your rightness or wrongness?
- What if you no longer needed to be right or wrong?
- Who could you be and how much energy would you have available to truly create your life?

Tool: Interesting Point of View I Have This Point of View

From alignment and agreement, or resistance and reaction, you can move into allowance by saying, "Interesting point of view I have this point of view"—even if you have to say it a hundred times before you actually get there.

Initially, the alignment and agreement, or the resistance and reaction, may seem locked in. But as you continue to say to yourself, out loud or in your head, "Interesting point of view I have this point of view," you'll notice that it begins to unlock and shift. You're saying, "I'd like to be in allowance about this. I'm not there yet, but I'm getting closer." Keep saying, "Interesting point of view I have this point of you" as often as required until you cannot find that point of view anymore. It's only your alignment, agreement, resistance, or reaction that keep your points of view from dissipating. You don't need to meditate many hours a day to be in allowance, but you do need to use this tool. It begins with a choice—and it takes practice.

The Space of Allowance

When you are in allowance and permit yourself to know what you know, you don't buy the garbage people are selling in this reality. For example, are you someone who thinks you don't have enough money? Many of us say, "I don't have enough! I don't have this and that!"

Consider this: You *do* have enough. You're simply not willing to know how much you have because you have aligned and agreed with other people's points of view. You're not yet willing to know how much you have that does not align with this reality.

What naturally stems from the space of allowance is a different possibility. When you look at something and say, "Isn't it interesting that someone would choose this," you open the door to asking,

- What can I choose?
- What can I choose that would be different?
- What can I choose that would contribute to a different possibility?

When you are in allowance, you are being *you* all the time, and you become an energy that inspires people.

Clearing: Living *From*, *As*, and *With* Awareness and Knowing

What have you made so vital and definitive about life that keeps you from creating a life that is living from, as, and with awareness and knowing? Everything that is, will you destroy and uncreate it all? Right and Wrong, Good and Bad, All 9, POD and POC, Shorts, Boys, and Beyonds.

What if you are the space for, and the voice for,
something totally different on this planet?

THE JOY OF JUDGMENT OR THE JOY OF AWARENESS:

WHICH DO YOU CHOOSE?

Most people think that knowing is a kind of completion rather than the beginning of a different possibility. They think that the wisps of awareness occurring from moment to moment have no value. This way of thinking leads to the stultification of this reality.

It is *way more exciting* to be aware, and have possibilities show up all the time, than it is to get stuck in time and place with judgments, answers, completions, and conclusions. How many times have you thought, "As soon as I have an answer, I'll be done with this"? You have defined knowing as an *answer* instead of a *possibility*. When you do this, you do not allow yourself your own knowing.

This happened with Einstein. He did his thing with the theory of relativity and went into conclusion about how right he was. Then, other people started coming up with quantum mechanics, but Einstein was already satisfied with an answer and a solution. He wasn't willing to be so much more in a way that would make everybody extend themselves to create more realities.

The Joy That Awareness Gives You

Awareness has nothing to do with reaching a conclusion, taking control, judging, or figuring things out. It's about knowing in the moment and asking questions. It's the space where you say, "This is what I know," and a world of choice, question, and contribution opens up. A totally new set of possibilities becomes available to you.

Things move when you ask a question, and the constant movement creates different possibilities. When you put your attention on something without having reached any sort of judgment or conclusion about it, things change.

Total awareness gives us a sense of joy. The huge advantage of being totally aware is that you can look at things and see why they aren't working. Then, you choose what will work.

Conclusions, Results, Answers, and Completions

Conclusions, results, answers, and completions have nothing to do with consciousness because consciousness never completes. Consciousness simply continues to open more doors to more possibility. If you have any kind of result in mind about how something should look, you won't be able to receive a different possibility. When you

THE JOY OF JUDGMENT OR THE JOY OF AWARENESS

have already concluded what's supposed to happen, you aren't able to receive possibilities. Conclusion kills possibilities.

Rather than receiving something with ease and awareness, you say, "I don't like this." Is that a question? No. You are doing conclusions and decisions. You don't ask,

- What can I create with this?
- What can I do with this?
- How can I play with this?
- How can this work for me?
- What will it lead to if I choose this?
- What will this produce?

What have you made so vital about the wrongness of awareness that keeps you from the joy that awareness gives you?

We were talking about this with an attorney who asked, "Are you saying that I have to completely eliminate all conclusions?"

"Yes," Gary said. "I know that must be hard for a lawyer who is planning to be a judge."

The attorney asked, "Do you have any tips on how to do that in daily life?"

"For starters," Gary told him, "when you realize that people can't hear what you are saying, shut up. When you shut up, especially if you're an attorney, people are going to tell you all kinds of stuff."

The attorney said, "I know. It is difficult to listen to all that stuff."

"That's the lie you are buying," Gary said.

Susanna offered, "You told us about a dinner you had with a guy in real estate. Didn't you just shut up and let him say whatever he needed to say? How much information did you get from that?"

"Yes, actually I did do that and got a lot of information. It was fun. Are you saying I can create fun with this kind of situation?"

Exactly. It *is* fun to live as question, awareness, and knowing. Don't try to fill empty space. Leave it open; the space will fill itself. When you have space, you can have total awareness.

Moving Beyond Interpretation

The greatest kindness you can be to yourself, others, and the world is to avoid functioning from any form of judgment and interpretation. The greatest kindness in the world is allowing yourself to be aware, to know what you know, and to see what is, as it is, with no interpretation, no judgment, and no point of view.

A woman told us about a conversation she had with a friend. She said, "My friend pointed out that with the questions I was asking, I was not looking at the greatness of me. He was right. It seems like I'm doing something weird here — I'm happy to look at the lie I'm telling myself so I can get to the truth."

When you say you are happy to look at the lie in order to determine the truth, you are interpreting what is a lie and what is true. That's not what you want to do. It's not the *truth* you want; it's *awareness*. You're trying to figure things out, or interpret them, or judge them. That's like looking at limitations in order to get to freedom. You are not actually choosing freedom.

Everything that comes out of your mouth or out of your head is what you are creating in your life. Every single thought you have, everything you say, creates the life you have. If you are not happy with your life, you'd better listen to what you are thinking and saying because that is what is creating your life.

When you use your mind to interpret what you are aware of, you're not focusing on what actually *is*. You're focusing on something that *is not what is*. For example, some people try to interpret what other people's facial expressions or body language mean. They say, "This facial expression means x, y, z." They are interpreting things through a filter of their conclusions, which are not real and not true, in order to determine what is happening for them.

Using your mind to interpret does not lead you to knowing what is truly possible. You're making everything about you. For example, if there's some weird energy in the room, you might think, "I must have done something wrong. It must be my fault." When you do this, you cannot be the source of creation. You are making another person's behavior or their energy — and your interpretation of it — the source of creation. This doesn't lead you to what is possible or what is true for you.

You may think, "Well, if I make something my fault and I change it, I can control the situation." That's what they teach you as a kid. We are trained to do this in our childhood. But this is not the freedom that comes from awareness.

There is a level of freedom available to you when you are not at the effect of interpretation. Unfortunately, many mainstream psychologists use tools that were handed down by their universities, where everything is about interpretation, cognition, and the process of thinking. That takes so much work! It takes so much energy. And it never gives you the freedom to change.

Interpretation Keeps You from Being Present With What Is

Susanna did a lot of psychotherapy sessions with clients when she was working in mental health. She used cognitive behavioral therapy and psychodynamic approaches, and in her education she was trained to interpret what her clients said. She was taught that everything clients said and did — every way they moved and held their bodies — *meant* something. She realized early on that interpreting her clients kept her from being present with what is.

When your mind gets occupied with interpretations according to a certain theory you read in a book, you go back to that book and filter what is being said through past experience and knowledge rather than being present with what is. You miss so much!

Now, with Pragmatic Psychology, Susanna listens not only to what people *say* — she is also aware of *every nuance of energy* in order to catch the very moment when a problem can be turned into a possibility.

Clearing: Interpreting Energies That Cannot Be Translated

What have you made so vital about understanding meaning that keeps you eternally interpreting the energies that cannot be translated? Everything that is, will you destroy and uncreate it all? Right and Wrong, Good and Bad, All 9, POD and POC, Shorts, Boys, and Beyonds.

The greatest kindness you can be to yourself, to others, and to the world is to avoid functioning from judgment and interpretation.

5

THE EXTREME SPORT OF AWARENESS

Intensity is the form of living most desired on this planet. We think this is why people do extreme sports. They say, "When I do extreme sports, I am intensely alive. The closer I come to death, the more intensely alive I am." Extreme sports create an emergency situation, providing the only time they are willing to be true space and everything they are. They say it's orgasmic living. Some get to the point where they can only achieve that sense of intense aliveness when they are doing extreme sports.

What If You Could Enjoy Being Totally Present in Each Moment?

Once, in an Access class, we watched a video of one of the participants jumping out of a hot air balloon. He talked about the space of being there, the utter joy of just going for it, and the orgasmic energy of saying, "I'm going to fall now."

What would it be like if you were willing to have the utter joy of all possibility in all areas of your life, all the time, not just when you're in a hot air balloon? What if you could have that energy all the time, everywhere? What if you could enjoy being totally present in each moment?

For example, both of us love to ride horses. When we ride, we know we have to be totally present with the horse. We cannot check out. We cannot be stupid. We cannot be unaware. When you are willing to be that intensity of presence in every moment of every day, your awareness becomes so intense that you may not be able to tolerate it at first. That's okay. You simply need to ask, "What is possible here?" and *be* in that question.

Once you go to the question, everything becomes possible. It is the speed of space. It is the awareness of being. Yes, it is intense and uncomfortable — because awareness is not always comfortable.

If you are willing to have the intensity of total awareness, you end up with an intensity that is greater than extreme sports, greater than great sex, greater than great food. Awareness exponentializes all of those things so they become even greater. When you do extreme sports, have great sex, or eat great food from the intensity of your awareness, they are even more fun — not because *they* are the source of the intensity but because *you* are. What if your intensity of awareness was greater than the intensity of anything else you could have?

An Intense Level of Receiving

One of our class participants had repeatedly injured herself while doing extreme sports.

"I recently blew out my knee snowboarding," she told us. "Right before I fell, I was thinking, 'This is awesome! I'm having such a good time.' I was experiencing the joy of awareness. It was incredible. I was just being the space."

Gary said, "And what were you aware of in that moment that created the accident? When you have that kind of extreme awareness, you are aware of everything that is happening. For example, people will look at you and think, 'Oh my God! She is going to fall.' Maybe someone watching you had the point of view, 'If I did that, I would die!' Maybe you 'heard' the 'I would die,' and assumed it was your point of view, so you weren't aware that point of view was coming from someone else. You didn't get that. You didn't see it coming. You have to have an intense level of receiving at all times — so when somebody projects something like that at you, you don't have to fall. You don't have to have an accident."

"Well, yes," the woman said, "but there were whiteout conditions. The conditions were really bad. I shouldn't have been going that fast."

"Whose point of view was that?" Gary asked.

The woman's eyes widened. "Oh! Yes! I get it! That was the point of view of the people around me at the moment I went flying past."

"When you are in those extreme situations," Gary said, "you are open to receiving everything. Unfortunately, you didn't get that in addition to everything else you were aware of; you were receiving the projections and expectations of everyone around you. They were heavy, but you weren't experiencing them as heavy at the moment because you were receiving totally, and when you are receiving totally, things are not heavy."

Be aware that others cannot receive what you can do. This applies to any area of your life, especially your talents. That snowboarder was intensely open to receiving, but she bought other people's projections and expectations as hers. They impinged on her world. It could have played out differently; she could have received the projections and expectations and said, "Oh, that's not relevant to me," and she would have been fine.

The Ability to Choose More

When you increase your awareness, you are on the extreme edge of everything you do, rather than slugging through life like most people. You have the ability to choose more, or not, as you wish. When you are willing to have that intensity of awareness, you exponentialize the joy of what you're doing.

When Gary does extreme horse riding, he knows he has to be intensely aware. If he's not, he's going to create a problem, or the horse will. You want that intensity of awareness because it gives you total receiving and opens the doors to everything possible in life that you have never been able to achieve.

Susanna loves to go downhill skiing. She loves speed. The surface of the mountain changes with every meter, so she has no choice but to be extremely aware of her body, the mountain, the surface, what is going on around her with other skiers, and what is coming ahead. She has to receive it all. That level of receiving invites you to a greater level of being. It's being the orgasmic uncontrollable bundle of joy you truly are!

Right now, perceive everything around you, every molecule, and allow it in. What are you noticing? There is no right or wrong answer to this. Do it again. What are you noticing now? Things are never the same from moment to moment. There is no need to control anything. Practice receiving. You can do this anywhere and at any time. No fitness studio is needed.

What if your intensity of awareness was greater than the intensity of anything else you could have?

6

CHOOSING MORE: CHOICE MAKES LIFE AN ADVENTURE

Choice is the beginning of all creation. However, most people — instead of choosing more in their lives or choosing what works for them — try to justify their choices. They say, "I chose this *because*..." Every time you say *because*, you stultify yourself. You're not actually choosing. You're trying to justify your choice or prove that choosing it was a good thing. You're not being pragmatic. The pragmatic choice is to choose for you. When you choose for you, you know you're always going to get what you want.

Choosing for you can be challenging at first. Others may not agree. For example, we had someone sign up for an Access seven-day event in Costa Rica. Her manager did not approve, but she was still choosing to go. Gary offered some advice:

"Tell your manager, 'I would really like to be better at my job. I would like to be more productive and create even more, so I'm choosing to do this. You can dock my pay or do whatever you need to do. If you want to fire me, that's fine, too, because I know I will get a great job after I do this class.' Or you could say, 'If you don't really want me here, this is your opportunity to get rid of me, because if I get better at my job, I will out-create you and steal yours.'

Gary paused and said, "Actually, you should just *think* that second one. Don't say it. That's pragmatic psychology. You are aware of what people need to hear, and you use your awareness for you and what you've chosen. You say what your boss needs to hear, not as a stultification but as a creation, as a possibility."

Choose and See What Happens

Every time you choose, something shows up in your life because of that choice. You may not realize it, but when you choose something, you have already looked at it and said, "Okay, I can have this. I can receive this." Most people choose based on what they can receive with ease. But you also have to be willing to choose what you don't think you can receive with ease.

The only reason you can't receive something is because you have decided it is too uncomfortable. It is always about what you have *decided* you can't receive. But you have to learn to choose that, too, because it is never about what you *truly can't* receive. This is where we create the greatest inroads to change the parts of our lives we most desire to change.

Here's an important question: Do you have to already know what works for you in order to be able to create it?

The answer is, you might be *aware* of some things that work for you, but how many times have you tried to come to conclusion about what works, rather than having the adventure of finding out? Choose and see what happens. Choice creates awareness. We *can* make life an adventure, not a predetermined reality.

When something isn't working for you, or when everything isn't working the way you want, know that there is something blocking you—something you are not willing to be or are not willing to receive. Ask, "What am I not willing to be or receive that keeps this from working for me?"

Being Pragmatic Is Embracing All Choices

One of our students said to us, "I notice times when my awareness expands so much that it seems like I use that awareness against me rather than for me."

When that happens to any of us, we can just say, "All right. Enough! I'm not doing this anymore. I am choosing something different."

We also must be aware of the places we love that we keep choosing again and again. The problem is, we often do not stop choosing the places we love *even when they no longer work for us*. When you screw yourself over by choosing those places, you think it proves how powerful you are because you can pull yourself up by your bootstraps, get on with it, and turn things around.

Maybe you could acknowledge the fact that you are powerful. Then, you don't have to bother proving it to yourself.

Choose and see what happens. Choice creates awareness. You need to make life an adventure, not a predetermined reality.

7

WOULD YOU LIKE TO HAVE MORE MONEY?

Would you like to increase the amount of money that flows into your life? If so, we invite you to start tithing to the church of *you*. We're talking about putting aside 10 percent of every dollar that comes in for *you*. You pay yourself first. When you do this, you're telling the universe that you deserve money — and more money will start to show up for you.

Putting away 10 percent for *you* is the opposite of meanness. One definition of meanness is a lack of generosity. Meanness is greediness or miserliness or penny-pinching; it's being super economical or frugal; it's re-using a tea bag in order to save money. Meanness is the place where you make something the smallest amount you can receive as if that's going to create greater possibility in your life. It never will.

Start Paying You 10 Percent Before You Pay for Anything Else

When you begin to put 10 percent away for you, you create more money coming into your life. Consider what happens by *not* paying yourself first. If you say, "First, I'm going to pay all my bills," what do you usually get? More bills. Is that what you want? Or would you like to have more money?

If it's more money you desire, start paying *you* first. You may have to adjust for a few months, stretching out bills before you get used to paying yourself 10 percent first, but you can do it.

It's 10 percent of the gross, not the net. Don't try to weasel out of it!

But don't do it because we're telling you to do it. That won't work because as soon as you get into a financial bind you'll spend the money. And then you'll say, "Argh! I have no money again!" Set aside 10 percent as a way of honoring you. Do it because it's pragmatic.

Wow, I Have Money!

As you continue to put 10 percent away, there will come a time when you will have a certain amount of money, whatever that amount is for you — it's a different amount for each person — and you'll say, "Wow, I have money!" You will have a sense of security about money, and you will no longer think about it nearly as much.

We talked with a woman who, many years earlier, had started a 10 percent account for her business income. She told us that her husband had recently started his own 10 percent account as well. She said that their income had increased significantly — to the point that she was now setting aside *almost 100 percent* of her income.

She told us, "A few months ago, I started to put close to 100 percent of my income into my 10 percent account so I could create even more magic. But with that change, we didn't have enough money at the end of the month to pay all of our bills. We started to borrow money in order to survive. My husband's point of view is that I am spending too much."

Why wasn't her financial situation improving? Her husband was fixated on the money that *wasn't* there rather than the money that *was* there. He was willing to honor his bills. But when you honor your bills over yourself, your *bills* grow. When you honor *you*, your *finances* grow. That's why we suggest putting away 10 percent first. One hundred percent will obviously be too much for nearly everyone. If you are able to save 10 percent of your income for you, your financial situation is improving because maybe you weren't putting anything away previously.

The Space of Money

Money allows you to have space. People who have money have lots of space around them — big houses and big offices and big seats on airplanes.

Some people have what we call "space phobia." They are not comfortable with space, and they're always trying to fill it up. They do this by thinking, eating, emoting, feeling, or creating a new relationship that doesn't work for them. Why do they do that? So they can feel "normal" and just like everyone else.

People do the same thing with money. They don't want to have the space that extra money creates. They want to have the fear or they want to have the poverty, which creates the density that lets them know everything is "real."

We're looking for the space of money—the space where you know you have money, where you are looking for what is available. If you know you have money, what will you choose? For each of us, there is a certain amount of money we know we must have in order to feel truly secure.

- What would it take for you to know you have money?
- What constitutes money for you?

Our friend Simone was teaching a class about money and asked the participants, "How much money would you have to have in order to know you have money?" Somebody said, "Eight thousand five hundred dollars per month." Another person may have been thinking, "I must be doing better than I thought because I already make more than that."

It's different for everyone. What about you? How is your reality about money created? It's your point of view that creates your reality — *not* your reality that creates your point of view. If you think $8,500 per month is a lot of money, you will only let yourself have less than that, rather than the *more* that might be possible. You won't ask, "What else can I have?"

Using Money to Create a Future

A class participant once asked us, "I've been accused of spending a lot of money. What does it mean to spend?"

"People often tell me that I spend too much," Gary replied, "but

I don't *spend* money. I *use* money to create a future. I buy things like antiques and jewelry knowing that I'm creating a future in which I have wealth and money. I know that I'm spending to create a future."

You have to look at this and ask, *What does it mean to me when I spend? What's the future potential of my purchases?*

When you're considering spending money on something, you've got to ask what it is going to create for the future. Let's say you are putting a heating system into your house. That's a necessity. Do you put in the best heating system you can find, or the cheapest? If you choose the best one, you're creating a future where, when it gets really cold, you will still be fine.

Or, let's say you're putting in new floors. Do you buy the best and most beautiful floors, or do you buy ones that are just okay and cost a lot less? Many people say, "I'd choose the less expensive floors."

But why are floors not a necessity the way heat is? What's your justification? Do you think expensive floors are a luxury? You have defined beautiful floors as a luxury, and you won't spend money for the luxury of your life. You will only spend money on the necessities that keep you surviving. A lot of people have this point of view. They think it's wrong to spend money on comfort. But if you are not willing to spend on the luxuries of life, you are not willing to believe that you deserve luxury. Therefore, you will never create it in your life. How does that create a future in which you have wealth and luxury?

Make a Demand

Many years ago, when Gary was married and his wife was pregnant with their daughter, they weren't making enough money. At the age of forty-nine, Gary was not able to pay his mortgage and had to ask his mother to borrow $4,900 so they wouldn't lose their house.

Gary reflected on this difficult time: "My wife's attitude was that she didn't need to spend less; I had to earn more. My self-judgment was *I am only worth something if I earn enough*, so I worked to earn as much money as I could. But it was never enough. Having to ask my mother for money was the most embarrassing moment of my life."

He resolved to never again ask his mother for money. The next time there was a bill he couldn't pay, Gary sold something they owned, an antique, to get the $1,400 they needed to pay the bill. From his point of view, it was the pragmatic thing to do, but the item he sold was one of his wife's favorite antiques, and she never forgave him for selling it. She was only willing to look at the situation in terms of how she wanted it to be.

Finally, Gary got it. He made a demand: "This is never going to happen again. We are going to have money." That demand changed everything.

Making a demand is being willing *to go to any lengths* to change. It's saying, "I am not going to live like this anymore. No matter what it looks like, no matter what it takes, I am changing this!" You can follow up the demand with a question: "What is it going to take for me to have that?" With the demand and the question, you are asking the universe to contribute to you — and it will.

Susanna's approach to her finances was very utilitarian until she learned about making a demand. She had always had enough money to pay her bills. Her point of view was, "Why have more money than I need? What's the point?" Then she started working with Access Consciousness. For the first time in her life, she understood the value of money in terms of being able to change the world. She understood that to bring something into the world, one needs money. She saw that publishing a book, creating a webpage, and traveling to do workshops all require money. She made the demand of herself to have more money than she needed, and her life changed completely.

Everything you do can be about the consciousness you are going to create. When you are creating a future, spending money, or making a demand, it's about the consciousness you are going to create. When you look at what you want to create in the world, one option is to ask, "What can I do to have more of this reality?" We propose asking a different question: "What can I do that will contribute to consciousness?"

How is your reality about money created?
It is your point of view that creates your reality.
It is not your reality that creates your point of view.

8

THE EASE AND JOY OF LIVING

Some people see opportunities in everything around them. We know a realtor, for example, who has an amazing sense of how to create money. She told us she couldn't wait to find people who have the same mindset on the creation of money.

Gary asked her, "Do you actually think there are people who have the same mindset for creating money that you have? Do you actually believe that is true?"

The realtor said, "When I talk to people, I say, 'We can do this one deal and make $50,000. We don't have to do five different deals to make that kind of money.' But most of my clients aren't able to see that that is possible."

"You have the capacity to see possibilities that other people can't see," Gary told her. "You want to create — and big."

"That's true," the realtor replied. "Sometimes I work with people who are content with making 12 percent on their investments. When I start talking about doing something big, they can't even grasp it."

This realtor is trying to present a reality to those people that simply doesn't exist for them. Most people get a certain amount of money, and, once they get that amount, whatever it is for them, they think they no longer have to create. They think they can always survive. Is that enough for you?

- What about becoming someone who asks, "Why would I ever need to just survive?"
- Are you not willing to acknowledge that you are capable of succeeding to a degree other people will never even be aware of?
- What if you always knew that if you were to start over tomorrow, you would always succeed, wherever you went, whatever you did?

Many of us grew up with a utilitarian point of view. *Utilitarian* means functional, useful, practical, plain, and sensible — all in terms of this reality, of course. Utilitarian is never having more than you can handle. It's always having just enough. Nothing can be wasted and nothing can be abundant. Were you taught that you needed to be utilitarian about things?

Utilitarian means you could wear a burlap bag. Granted you might look great in a burlap bag, but silk would definitely be an improvement.

When Susanna first started to create enough money to travel around the world and do workshops, she used to travel economy class. Her point of view was, "This is good enough. Who needs business class?" It never even occurred to her to *not* fly economy class. It wasn't anything she desired. On long flights, she was often able to get a row of unoccupied economy class seats so she could lie down, and she was happy.

One day, after facilitating a Pragmatic Psychology class in Pretoria, South Africa, she was offered an upgrade to business class on a flight to Europe. Her first reaction was, "I don't need this." Then she paused. After a moment, she asked, "Even if I don't *need* this, what would it create if I chose it?"

Her world lit up. She suddenly perceived the joy that upgrading to business class would create in the present and in the future. The moment she sat down in the large, business-class seat, she felt her whole world expand and her future change. She understood that going with what you *need* is one thing, but choosing what brings you and your body *joy*, going for hedonism, expands your world even more than you can imagine.

The Planet Is Hedonistic and Abundant Beyond Belief

You may have bought the lie that opulence, hedonism, and decadence can't coexist with the sustainability of the planet. Have a look at that idea. Is it true? How hedonistic is the planet? How abundant is it?

- The Earth is incredibly productive. This planet is hedonistic and abundant beyond belief. When there is enough water, the Earth grows more seeds. And when you have

enough money, you grow more possibilities.
- Are you functioning as though there is a lack in you that you must fill?
- How much energy are you using to create the lack in you that you keep trying to fill with a relationship, food, or thoughts?
- Do you fill your head with thoughts all the time? And your heart with feelings?

What Would You Do If Your Life Was Total Ease?

Most people think they have to have a problem to solve in their lives. They can't imagine what they would do if their life was total ease. What would you do if your life was total ease? We asked that question during a class.

One woman said, "The answer I got was, 'I would have fun.' But I don't know what that means."

Think about what she said: "I would have fun, but I don't know what that means." This implies she *can't* have fun because she doesn't know what it means. Instead, all she can have is a problem, which always gives her something to overcome.

Were you raised with this sort of utilitarian point of view? Did you go into alignment and agreement with it? Would you be interested in beginning to unlock it with "Interesting point of view I have this point of view"?

Can You Have Everything You Desire?

Susanna was brought up like a princess. There are two kinds of princesses: A princess whose life looks like a fairy tale, where everything in the picture is just right, and the princess who knows she can have anything she desires. We're talking about the second kind of princess, the one who knows she can have anything she desires.

Susanna's parents showed her that everything is possible and that she could do everything she wished to do. That was a great kindness to her. She grew up knowing that every molecule in the universe was willing to contribute to her if she chose it.

Gary's parents, on the other hand, believed in the rightness of hard work. They raised him to be a pauper — someone who has nothing but knows he can get something if he works hard enough. They tried to convince him that he could *do* anything but not someone who could *have* anything.

A lot of parents do this. They're convinced hard work creates what one desires, so they motivate their kids to work hard. *Smart* work, however, is not part of their reality. And neither is being pragmatic. How were you raised? However it was, you have to ask,

- What part of how I was raised is actually true and real for me?
- What part of how I was raised is actually a lie?

Do you use your past as the reason and justification for why you don't have a choice? Or, instead, do you choose to ask, "What part of this can I use and how can I use it?" This would be the joy of awareness.

When you ask questions, you have an awareness of different directions things could go in the future. You have to ask questions — whether it's about business or a relationship or anything else — so you start to trust your knowing. Most people don't do this. They go directly to conclusion, which takes them out of productivity and creation and puts them into the stultification of this reality.

- Do you believe in hard work and do a lot of it?
- Have you always been smarter than your parents wanted you to be?
- Are you willing to have the gift of the willingness to have money?
- Do you believe there has to be an easier way?

If you are not willing to surpass your parents' point of view about money, you have accepted that what they have decided about money is true and real.

The Sense of *Wanting* or *Lacking*

Are you willing to acknowledge that money is everywhere and there is no shortage of it? It is the people who believe there is a shortage of money who create a lack of it in order to prove they are right in their limitation. In so doing, they guarantee that possibility is not a reality for them. Most people are not willing to have possibility as a reality. They are only willing to have possibility as a dream, a wish, a desire — a star they can count on. They're functioning from a sense that they *lack*.

People who function from a sense of lack are proving they have a lack and are right in their lack. One woman we worked with, her husband was doing this. She asked us, "What do I need to say to him so he will create more?"

We offered the idea that she could make him *right* in his lack instead of trying to change him. The woman told us she had been doing the opposite: "I have been trying to show him the possibilities," she said, "but it seems like he doesn't want that."

She was correct. He didn't want the possibilities. He had already decided that reality is, "I will lack." We cannot make people change. We can accept their reality while living our own and creating more possibilities.

Want Is Not a Real Word

When you grow up in a family that has money, *want* is not a real word. It's a fake word, a pretense of a word, a word that does not really exist. Families who are not dedicated to *lack* or *want* tend to give lip service to it. They may talk about *want* as though it is true, but they don't actually believe it.

When you grow up in a family that *wants*, your whole focus in life is about what you lack. You make *want* and *lack* true. You have the point of view that you have to have lack in order to receive. Your motivation for creation is your lack. You assume that you lack when you don't think you are the source for the creation of money.

So many people are amazing at creating. They create what works for them or what creates more, yet too often they keep returning to a sense of lack. They haven't yet recognized what they are capable of and what they are creating.

What Haven't You Acknowledged That You Are Actually Capable Of?

The realtor we spoke of earlier creates huge amounts of money through real estate. She doesn't *make* money; she *creates* it — and she acknowledges that she does so. It's a great benefit to acknowledge what you create.

Many people don't do this. They have the point of view, "If I just post this information on the Internet, if I just advertise this class, if I just throw this item out into the world, if I do all this kind of stuff, that is enough." But it's not enough. It's not just about posting information or advertising a class or throwing something out into the world. It's about creating and recognizing what you are capable of. What haven't you acknowledged that you're actually capable of? This is a question you must make sacrosanct in your universe: "What haven't I acknowledged that I'm actually capable of?"

Celebrate Creation

The twist here is how easy it is to acknowledge everything you are and everything you have created. How do you do that? You look at what you create and you say, "I created this! This thing is beautiful." The party you could throw is huge, but you're not joining the party. You are standing on the street outside the party, asking, "When is somebody going to invite me in?"

You think you want people to see you, hear you, care for you, and love you. You *think* you want all that stuff — rather than realizing that when you celebrate creation, you will be demanded of with such intensity that you will be required to reach into the deepest, darkest depths of your reality to create and choose to do things you have never done before.

But you don't do that. You hide from you. You make yourself believe that you don't have these abilities and capacities...but based on what? Why would you do that? We all have the ability to choose things other people haven't chosen, but so often we don't acknowledge it.

When you are demanded of and it feels difficult, look for what is possible. Ask,

- What do I need to do?
- What do I need to deliver?
- What is going to create — and what is not?

When you do this, you will know what creates what. You will know what will be created by each choice. And it doesn't matter where you go. The direction you choose is just a choice. You can choose again and again and again.

Creating the Judgment of Wealth

When you have money and wear something flashy, it's easy to imagine how others may be judging you. Recently, Gary considered wearing three rings instead of his usual two. The third one is set with a seriously huge diamond. He knew people would look at him and say, "That guy has money," or "That guy needs all the external stuff he's wearing in order to feel good about himself." Either way, it would be a judgment. And what would that judgment do? Two things: First, it would diminish what the judging person could have. Second, it would increase what Gary could have — but only if he had no point of view about it. That's the key thing: *if he had no point of view about it*. When you know what judgment you are creating, you are the leader in that moment.

Have you ever walked into a room and noticed that you've contracted and gone into someone else's judgmental world? Here's something about judgment you may not realize: If you create the right kind of judgment in other people, it can actually get you more money. They may be thinking, "That guy has money," or "That guy needs all that external stuff," but they're judging only because that diamond ring is not part of most people's reality. When you create the judgment of wealth, you become wealthier, because people will put great amounts of energy onto the fact that you are wealthy. Notice that they turn their judgment into a *fact*.

When people judge you, acknowledge what they are doing. Say, "Thank you for the judgment." There is nothing wrong with being judged. It just means you get to make more money. Instead of going to, "That person is judging me and that's bad," start looking at what is real and true. You have to be willing to call a spade a spade. Judgments are conclusions intended to create limitations for you. You have to develop the willingness to recognize that a judgment is just a judgment; it's not a reality. And it can make you money!

Playing Creates Much More Money Than Work Does

Do you complain about having to work? Is "Oh, no, I have to do more work" something you say regularly? Most people work really hard, and one of the things they work the hardest at is trying to *not* be who they are. Let us ask you something: Are you an infinite being? Or are you a finite being who has to work really hard to get anything in life?

We like to work. For us, work is play. We enjoy what we do even more than vacations, which are actually kind of boring compared to what we get to handle when we work with people.

You have to learn to play with you and your body. You have to learn to play at creating money and play at doing work and play at whatever you do. Start acknowledging how much you like to play and see how many ways you can play to make more money.

When Susanna started her first business, she had the point of view that it would mean hard work all the time. Yet she had never believed in hard work, she began to fill every minute with something to do because she thought that was the way to make sure her business would not fail. After a while, she realized she was not having any fun with her business. She asked herself, "What made me choose to create a business?" The answer was, "The joy of it! So, what would I have to change to have the joy of business again?"

She realized that her point of view about work was in the way. She also realized that this point of view was not even hers in the first place; she had bought it from many other people in the business world.

She asked, "What do I know about business?" With that question, everything changed. She started to *play* business, like she did when she was a little girl and played shopkeeper. She stopped taking business seriously and making it "real." She started to ask, "What does my business require today?" She started to expand her knowing about when it was time to do something to move things forward. Sometimes it was calling somebody, sometimes it was taking care of emails, and sometimes it was taking a walk in nature or going horseback riding.

Clearing: Become a Playmate of Consciousness

What have you not acknowledged is true for you that, if you would acknowledge it, would allow you to be a playmate in the playground of consciousness and possibilities for all eternity? Everything that is, will you destroy and uncreate it all? Right and Wrong, Good and Bad,

All 9, POD and POC, Shorts, Boys, and Beyonds.

Life as Play

A participant in one of our classes told us about her parents, who were from Russia. They used to say to her that she had to get stuff done with her bum — by sitting and doing her schoolwork.

"There was no play," she said. "Play was only allowed if I did well in school."

Gary asked, "Don't you realize that school was play for you? You played at being a hard-working student, but you were so smart you could have just smiled and they would have given you an A."

"That's true," the woman replied. "I was so good at physics that even if I failed a test, the teacher would say, 'Come do this test again, because I know that you know this stuff better than anyone in the class.'"

She was *pretending* that school was not play for her. We do this all the time. We pretend things are hard; in reality, everything is play for us. Life is a theatre we orchestrate every day. We are the director of the symphony of possibilities.

Clearing: Become an Orchestrator of Possibilities

What orchestrator of possibilities are you that you haven't acknowledged? Everything that is, will you destroy and uncreate it all? Right and Wrong, Good and Bad, All 9, POD and POC, Shorts, Boys, and Beyonds.

When you know that you are the one who is choosing, you realize that when you make things hard for yourself *you* are the one choosing that. You see that your point of view creates your reality.

Susanna was once working with a man who said, "Everything in my life is great — except money. I never seem to be able to create money. This is the only area where I have troubles. I have not been able to change it."

"Who is creating this?" Susanna asked.

"I am."

"What is the value of creating this?"

"Hmm… Not being able to create money doesn't seem to have any value, but now that you ask, I realize it's something I have to do."

"What do love about having no money?"

The man laughed and said, "Wow, I never realized that I love having no money." He recognized that he chose to have no money because it defined who he was. As long as he had the problem of no money, he knew who he was.

"I must admit that makes me feel lighter," he said. "Realizing that I am only pretending to be a pauper."

What about you?

- Who would you be if you did not have problems?
- How much have you defined yourself over problems?
- Would you be willing to find out who you are beyond problems?
- Is it now time to play?

Never Enough Money but Always Too Much to Spend

One class participant told us that although she had recently switched jobs and was no longer working full-time, she was earning the same amount as before. She had come to the conclusion that it was good to be working halftime and making just as much money. But she hadn't yet asked,

- What else is possible I have never even considered?
- What is the thing that is going to put me over the edge — where I am making too much money and don't have to work more than I truly desire to work?

Each part of that becomes a choice — the work, the money, and the time. Another participant said, "I equate work, money, and time, too. I am up at 4:30 a.m. at the latest, and I work so much that I am always tired. What am I not doing?"

She was trying to equate what equals what rather than asking, "What would it take to get to…?" Or, "What would I like to do today to create more money than I could possibly handle?" Getting serious doesn't create money. What had this person made so vital about the seriousness of life that kept her from the joy and the ease of living?

We hear from a lot of students something along the lines of, "I have savings and investments, but it doesn't feel like enough." Does this sound like you? Here's what you want: Never enough money but always more than you can spend. It's okay if that's confusing at first. Your mind cannot logically compute that because it's a non-computable amount of money. If you try to compute it, you diminish it and limit it.

Ask, "What energy, space, and consciousness can my body and

I be today to generate, create, and physically actualize 'Never enough money but always too much to spend'?" This question puts out into the universe the point of view that you do not limit the amount of money you are willing to have. It's never enough, so more can come in; at the same time, you have so much that it's impossible to spend it all. You're saying, "I don't need money, as I already have more than I can spend, but I am open to receiving more."

You have to get the point of view that there is never enough — because that is the truth. For you, as a humanoid, there is ever enough. At the same time, you always have more available. You have more possibilities and more choices than other people have. You've always had more.

So, if you've always had more, what other choices are possible? This way of being totally goes against the utilitarian point of view of this reality and acknowledges the incredible abundance of the planet that is available to you if you choose it.

You may have bought the lie that opulence, hedonism, and decadence can't coexist with the sustainability of the planet.
Have a look at that idea.
Is it true?
How hedonistic is the planet? How abundant is it?

9

PUTTING THE PRODUCTIVE ELEMENTS OF LIFE INTO MOTION

The word *productive* brings up a lot for many people because they don't understand what *production* means and what pragmatic productivity is.

When you create something in the world, you are working with three elements: generation, creation, and institution. *Generation* is where you come up with the idea. *Creation* is putting the idea into existence. *Institution* is the production that creates something. Production happens out in the world. It is actualizing into existence that which has yet not existed.

When you are willing to be pragmatically productive, you have the idea (generation), you set something up (creation), and you put the lines of production in motion (institution). Then, things start to show up at a speed that works for you. Things fall into place, and you don't even know how it happened. You don't have to try to control anything. You put the productive elements of your life into motion and they continue to grow on their own. It's like getting a train moving. You might not see that it's moving at first, but suddenly it's on its way.

Once you are willing to be pragmatically productive, the lines of production continue to move even though you are no longer involved in them. A few years ago, for example, Access was in forty-seven countries. Now we are in 171. While Access was growing, people told us that we weren't doing all the correct things to get it out there the way we should. Yet, in six months, we doubled our mailing list — from 70,000 people to 140,000.

Here's another example: Gary started building The Antique Guild, his antique business in Brisbane, Australia, several years before it took off — but it did indeed take off. Today, it is known as the second best antique shop in Australia and is fast becoming the best. And he recently opened a second showroom in a historic building in another part of the city.

Similarly, Pragmatic Psychology started as a question in a small room in Sweden: "What else is possible with psychology that we have not yet considered?" Later, the first book about Pragmatic Psychology, *Practical Tools for Being Crazy Happy*, was published. It contained stories about Susanna's experience working with patients in mental health.

To her surprise, the book was so well-received that people started to ask for more. Workshops were created, and Susanna was invited to speak in different places around the world. The first Pragmatic Psychology Center — a place where people are acknowledged for what they know but have never expressed — has now opened in Vienna. Mental health conferences all over the world are now asking Susanna to speak about Pragmatic Psychology; she can barely keep up with the requests she receives. The moment Susanna stopped interfering in her creations, they started to bloom and take on a life of their own.

Producing vs. Doing

When we talk with people about being pragmatically productive, they often ask, "What is the difference between *producing* and *doing*?" *Doing* is about getting something done. It's about completion. *Producing* is about creating an ongoing reality that can be added to and subtracted from. Producing can include doing, but it doesn't necessarily have to be doing.

Many people are reluctant to produce. We wait for a relationship to show up or our ship to come in laden with riches. Or we just wait for *something* to happen. Are you waiting for something and have no idea what you are waiting for? Don't wait for anything! What if, instead of waiting, you became the productive speeding bullet of consciousness you truly are?

Create a More Productive Reality

Many people have the sense that they are not productive enough in their lives. They wonder if they just need to be more patient.

Remember that we are humanoids — people who see the possibilities in the world. Humanoids never feel they are productive enough because they know that so much more is available. This is a good thing, but it can have a challenging flip side: No matter what they are doing or what they have done, they feel they are never doing enough. Their mantra is, "I'm not doing enough." If you turned "I'm not doing enough" into "What else is possible?" you would create an even more productive reality. Start asking,

- What else can I produce?
- What else can I do?
- What else can I be?

Don't wait for anything! What if, instead of waiting, you became the productive speeding bullet of consciousness you truly be?

10

PRAGMATIC RELATIONSHIPS

When we talk with people about creating a different possibility on this planet, they often say that they're looking for *someone* to build with. They feel stultified and think that if they find a special person to work with them, they will be able to create.

A lot of women, for example, buy into the lie that being with a man is going to create something for them financially. This reality promotes the idea that if you don't have your other half, if you don't have a dog, if you don't have a cat, if you don't have children, if you don't have a white picket fence…you don't have what's good. One of the greatest stultifications in this reality is the idea that we *need* a man or a woman to have a relationship with in order to be complete.

We don't buy that idea. Why? Because we are all infinite beings. *You're* an infinite being. Think about that. Infinite beings don't become complete by having a relationship. Infinite beings become complete by making themselves infinite.

Trying to Fit Yourself Into the Relationship Box

It's a lie created by society that you lack something. It's a lie that you can't be great by yourself. A lie creates a place where no truth can be instituted and no change is possible. When you lie to yourself, you put a nail in your shoe. All you can do is go around in a circle over and over again, and the nail keeps digging into your foot. What if you created a different possibility instead?

The paradigm of relationship on this planet was never anything that had worked for Susanna. Her point of view was, "If relationship is something where people compromise parts of themselves to fit into the relationship box and then drift further and further apart from each other, I am not interested!"

But society has a different idea. When you are not in a relationship, you are made wrong for it. People would tell her things like, "You too will find somebody, don't you worry!" Even though she was clear that the relationship paradigm in this reality was not for her, she saw she was subtly making herself wrong for not having one.

She realized she was looking at what she *should* have according to this reality rather than looking at what she truly *desired*. Trying to be like others made her "right," but it also made her unhappy—and that wasn't good enough. So, she began to be in allowance for her desires even when they were "not right" in this reality. She asked herself,

- What do I truly desire?
- Who and what would truly be nurturing to me?
- What can I receive that I never thought I could receive?

She started to make what *she* desired more valuable than what is desirable in this reality. What showed up was totally different from what she expected. The universe presented her with a different kind of companion when Gary asked her if she wanted to buy one of his horses. A horse! The horse matched the energy of nurturing that Susanna desired at that time, and adding it to her life made everything expand.

As our colleague Dr. Dain Heer puts it, things never show up the way you think they will. One day, Susanna literally ran into somebody in a hotel, and he later became the unexpected man in her life. Like her beloved horse, he matched the energy of nurturing and expansion she was asking for.

- What if relationships were *creationships* and there to have fun with?
- What is possible for you today that was not possible yesterday?

A Relationship That Truly Works for You

People who are in great relationships are producing something that doesn't commonly exist in this reality. They're producing something that doesn't exist according to other people's standards.

But when you're stuck in the stultification of this reality, you are limited by the form, structure, and significance of things and by an idea of what everything is supposed to look like. Please know that form, structure, and significance are some of the biggest limitations that keep you from creating what's possible — not only in relationships but in everything you do.

There are infinite possibilities of how a relationship can be created. But if you desire a relationship that is truly pragmatic, which means a relationship that truly works for you, you have to go to question. You have to ask,

- What's out there?
- What's being presented here?
- What truly works for me?
- What's possible here that I haven't even considered?

You have to study what works for you. Many people ask, "What should I do when I have the awareness that something in my relationship isn't working for me?" We suggest asking a simple question: "What would *I* like to do?" The moment you go to question, you open up doors that you didn't even know existed.

This is very different from what we're taught in this reality. We're taught what exists and what doesn't. We're taught what can be done and what can't. We're taught what's possible and what isn't. Yet everything you've done that was brilliant was not done from what you were *taught*. It was done from what you *chose*, which was likely far outside of other people's realities.

Tool: Does This Work For Me?

One woman said that her boyfriend was always telling her that she was going to outgrow him and that she deserved better. She told us, "At the same time he doesn't make any move to change."

Gary offered some thoughts: "Your boyfriend is trying to make you prove that you won't leave him, that you won't outgrow him, that you won't desert him. And that's not control. Or is it? He *is* controlling you. Let me ask you a question: Does he want to change?"

"No."

"If you want something greater than what you currently have," Gary said, "you need to ask yourself, 'Am I willing to leave him because he refuses to change and become something greater?' You are buying the point of view that he is going to lose if you leave him. But is that true? He is not willing to create and become great. Is that the person you want to be with? It sounds like he is manipulating you."

Susanna asked the woman if the relationship was working for her.

"I don't know," she replied. "There are times when he drives me crazy."

"Okay, then," Gary said. "Just be willing to move on when it's time to move on. If you ran into a guy who was equally good in bed and had way more money, would you leave this guy? Truth? No! You would say, 'Oh, I don't want to hurt him!'"

What About Getting Pragmatic in Your Relationships?

Are you trying to avoid hurting people who are trying to stop you from being you? Are you trying to stop things from happening that you already know are going to happen?

"Does this work for me?" is a powerful question. But instead of asking that, we try to come to a conclusion or a result. We ask, "What *should* I do?" or "How *should* this look?" We try to institute elements of this reality rather than having the joy of awareness and asking whether something truly works for us.

What about getting pragmatic in your relationships? What about saying, "Am I willing to have fun with this? Yes. Cool." With that joy of awareness, you will know what else is possible when a different window of possibility opens up.

Trying to Make Someone Happy

Some people have the point of view that their partner has to do what they want in order for the relationship to work. If the partner buys that idea, they become less and less of who they are in order to make the other person happy. Trying to make someone happy is one of the biggest stupidities we buy. Why? Because you cannot make other people happy! People have to make themselves happy.

Besides, if you want to make someone happy, who do you have to begin with? You have to begin with an unhappy person. This is an example of the pragmatics of knowing. If you know that you want to make somebody happy, then whoever you choose is going to be somebody who is unhappy. Is this what you desire?

Your Awareness Creates a Place Where You Are Never Alone

Are you waiting for someone to validate the future for you? Are you waiting for someone who sees the future you see rather than being a person who sees the future for yourself and goes for it? Many people call this "creating with someone." You say, "I want someone to create the future with." This is co-dependence rather than co-creation.

Many people try to avoid aloneness. They have trouble being alone.

They say, "Oh, I'm so lonely!" But why would you not prefer to be alone? It's so comfortable. It's so easy. Why would being alone not become the most valuable product in your life?

Besides, when you're truly aware and you celebrate the joy of awareness, you're willing to realize that your awareness creates a place where you're never alone. There's no aloneness because you have the entire universe supporting you.

Love your alone time. Ask, "What energy, space and consciousness can I be to be as alone as I can truly be for all eternity?"

What about getting pragmatic about relationships?
What about asking,
"Am I willing to have fun with this? Yes. Cool."
With that joy of awareness, you will know what else is possible when a different window of possibility opens up.

11

PRAGMATIC PARENTING

Many parents we work with talk about how concerned they are about making their kids happy, or making up for what they perceived as a loss in their kids' world. We ask them, "Can you really make up for somebody else's loss? Can you really *make* somebody else happy?" When your kids have had a loss or feel sad, don't try to make them happy. Ask a question instead: "What energy, space, and consciousness can I be that will allow my kid to grow up to be whoever he or she desires to be with total ease?"

What If Your Choices As a Parent Are Not Wrong?

Many parents who are divorcing express concern about the effects of their divorce on their kids. In her work as a therapist, Susanna has met countless people whose parents were divorced. Most of them had bought the story that the cause of their current problems or troubles was their parents' divorce. But when Susanna asked them if their parents' actions had truly impacted their life and determined their future, they realized that their story was not a reality. It was just a point of view they had adopted.

Susanna would then ask them, "What gift to you was your parents getting divorced?" Many said that after their parents' divorce, they started to do what worked for them, they fought less with others, and they began to create their lives in unexpected ways. Some of them pointed out the advantages of having divorced parents. They said things like, "Well, after my parents divorced, I had two homes. I got special attention in school. I learned that one does not have to put up with a bad relationship. You can just change it. It's okay."

What if your choices as a parent are not wrong? And what if your child is not wrong for what he or she chooses?

Truth, Lies, and Secrets

In a class, we heard from a man whose wife had committed suicide. He told us about how he communicated to their children about what happened:

"When my kids' mother died, I told them everything. Although my family was in agreement with telling my kids the truth, they said, 'Just don't tell them the specifics.' But I wanted the kids to hear everything from me rather than picking up rumors in school or from other people's conversations, so I was clear in my communication about what their mother had chosen and why she chose it. It paid off in the long run because there is no weirdness around her death. There were no lies or secrets.

"When my kids and I went to went to see a psychologist in the first six months after my wife's death, the psychologist said, 'Whatever it is that you are doing with your kids, keep doing it. They don't need to be here unless something shows up at some point in the future.'"

That was a pragmatic psychologist. There is no right way of grieving; there is no set procedure to go through. If whatever you're doing works for you, you're doing the right thing. Do what works as long as it works.

The Biggest Gift Is the Truth

That was a pragmatic father in the example above. Telling his kids the truth was the biggest gift he could have given them. He spoke to them as the infinite beings they are, not as some kind of pathetic little creatures who couldn't handle the truth. When you don't trust kids' ability to deal with the truth, you are telling them they are less than you are. When you don't tell the truth or when you have secrets, innuendo and rumors start to come in the back door. Those things create separation between parents and children.

After talking with the father, a woman in the class said, "I did the opposite with my daughter. Her father was an alcoholic who abandoned us, and I lied to her about it. She's thirteen now. What can I do?"

Kids always know when you're lying. If you make lying to your kids a habit, when you try to give them your truth about something, or when you try to share with them something you think is good, they can't hear it because they have to interpret it through the lies you've told them.

But we can correct this.

"You can bring out the truth," Gary offered the woman who had lied to her daughter. "You can say, 'You know what? I lied about a lot of things to do with your dad because I was trying to protect you. I lied about this and I lied about this. Here is what was true.' That will validate your daughter in what she already knows."

Secrets Solidify Your Awareness

By offering information that is true for you rather than making it a secret, you bring awareness to a situation. When you lie to somebody or keep secrets from them, you automatically reduce their willingness to perceive. You create a place where they have to interpret everything from the lie you've told.

When you are a child or adolescent and what is happening is not explained to you — when *what's true* is not explained — it becomes a secret, and that secret does not draw out your awareness. It solidifies your awareness into a concrete box, and you begin to believe that your awareness has no value. All that's left to you is the choice of interpretation and the trap of thinking you don't know. You're forced to interpret what shows up through levels of meaning you have created. This has nothing to do with awareness.

We once had someone working for us in Access who lied regularly. Gary finally let her go, but, initially, he didn't tell people the reason he had fired her. When people started asking why she was gone, he thought, "I'm not going to cover up her stuff," so he told people it was because she had been lying.

Our other team members responded positively to being told the truth. They said things like, "That relieves me so much! I always knew she was lying, but I could never put my finger on it."

We all know so much, but we often keep secrets to protect what we know and maintain the status quo. All wars are created based on secrets. It's the secret stuff they have going on in the back room that creates a war. This is true of any war — whether it's a worldwide war or a fight with your family.

Breaking away from secrets can be transformative. The father whose wife killed herself looked at the situation he was in and chose to not keep secrets. He asked, "What am I going to tell my kids? What's going to work for my kids?" He chose to be honest: "I'm going to be truthful with them and tell them exactly what they need to know so they have total clarity."

Most people try to withhold that kind of information. But when it comes to something like suicide, withholding information can have lasting effects on children. Some kids end up in psychological counseling for the rest of their lives. Or they start taking medication and off they go in the direction of no possibility. Please don't try to define the possibility of what can be achieved. Trust that your children can handle the truth, and know that truth is much easier to handle than a lie.

Quality Time

A lot of parents have the point of view that in order to create a good relationship with their kids, they have to spend quality time with them. This can cause anxiety. For example, parents may feel that they're neglecting their children when they have to travel for their jobs.

Some fathers we've worked with say they feel guilty because they can find ways to spend time with their sons, usually through sports, but they can't seem to find ways to spend quality time with their daughters. They're caught up in the idea of *quality time*. But it's not about the *time* you spend with your kids — it's about what you are *being* when you are with them.

Instead of feeling guilty, what about getting pragmatic and asking some questions?

- What if the time you spend with your kids each day is time when you are totally present?
- What are you already gifting your kids that goes beyond time?
- What if it is not about time at all? What are you being now, in the moment, when you are sitting with your kids?
- What are you gifting your kids that you haven't acknowledged?

Ask Your Kids Questions

You need to ask yourself questions and you need to ask your kids questions, too. Years ago, when Gary's children were in pre-school, the school instructed parents to not allow their children to watch television, especially an animated show called "He-Man: Masters of the Universe." Why not? Because the school said it created violence in the children.

Gary's kids liked that show a lot, so he sat down with them to ask about it: "What do you get out of this show? What is it you like about it? What do you think it is telling you? Does it make you feel like you need to go out and hit people?"

The kids responded, "Why would we go out and hit people, Dad?

That makes no sense. The show is about being aware of what happens after you do those things. You find out what hitting people causes."

What?! This was not what they had told Gary in the pre-school.

Another instruction from the school was to give boys dolls to play with, so that parents weren't indoctrinating boys into trucks and being a man's man. The only problem with that advice was that Gary's son loved trucks from the time he was a tiny baby. Once, when his son was just a few months old and they were in a toy store, the boy threw himself out of his stroller onto a toy truck. That little boy knew what he wanted. And what does he drive today? The biggest truck you have ever seen in your life. He loves that truck!

Questions Enable You to Find Out What Is Going On

We worked with a woman whose baby was constantly crying. The woman asked, "What should I do? What is wrong with my child? And what is wrong with me for not being able to make him stop crying?" Those may look like questions, but they are not. Those "questions" assume that something is wrong; that's a conclusion and a dead end.

We suggested that she ask her baby questions:

- What do you need?
- Do you need food?
- Do you need your diapers changed?
- Do you need me to hold you?
- Do you need anything else?

The mother would ask a question and wait for a moment to see how her baby responded. When she asked the question that matched what the baby was trying to tell her, he suddenly stopped crying. It is truly incredible what gets created when we ask and listen.

Child Rearing

People often talk about rearing children. But how many successful parents have you met who do child rearing? Zero. Why? Because you don't *rear* children. You don't train them. You don't prepare them for a job. You just try to love the little rascals. And when you love them, they get to do whatever they want.

You may think that loving them is teaching them how to not be screwed up, but that's not a very pragmatic point of view. Many parents get their children to stand in line and do all the things they are supposed to in this reality. They teach them to fit in and be like everyone else.

Did you follow everything your parents told you? Of course not. But you probably didn't rebel against it, either. You just didn't tell them everything. Becoming a teenager is the point in life in which you learn to lie, especially to the people who love you.

Your parents probably didn't want to hear what your point of view was, did they? They just wanted you to do what they decided was good for you so that they could prove they had good kids.

Gary's approach to parenting is different. "I don't have good kids," he says. "I have kids who do exactly what they want. And no matter how much I try to help them, they refuse my help."

Parents sometimes tell us, "I want to let my kids know that I have their back *and* that they can't just use me any way they want to. How can I show them that I have their back?"

Gary explains it this way: "Look, your kids *do* just want to use you. So let them use you. My kids taught me that I had no control over them. When they were about to make a mistake, I would say, 'This is going to turn out badly if you do it.' They would say, 'I know what I am doing. I don't need you, Dad.'"

When you allow your children freedom, they know you have their back. With that foundation, they have the confidence to explore the world and create endless possibilities for themselves.

Give Up Control

Trying to alter people's behavior doesn't work. Do you want to do what's easy for you? Or do you want the difficulty of trying to train somebody who doesn't want to be trained?

Saying to your children "I'm not going to support you in this" is trying to control things. You're trying to control them with money, which doesn't work. For years, parents have been trying to control their kids by cutting them off. In the 1960s, the idea of "tough love" was born. Parents practiced tough love so their kids would learn about the consequences of their actions. Some kids would go out and destroy themselves to make their parents wrong for having been tough.

Gary knew a guy who had a baby when he was fifty-five. He gave the child anything he wanted. His friends would say, "You're spoiling this kid. He's going to end up becoming a rotten egg." The man answered, "Maybe, but by the time he's a rotten egg, I'll be dead."

Why do we assume that spoiling children makes them rotten? You have to look at the situation and ask, "Is refusing to give them money going to make them change?" No, it's not. Give up control. Give up money. Give up the stultification of trying to control people's behavior through money. That's all this reality. Give it all up and move on.

Family

One lady said to us, "When you talk about allowance, I see the stupidity of my family. I can have some allowance for the stupidity of other people, but being in allowance of my own family is not so easy. I'm not willing to have them be stupid."

The greatest stultification in this reality is the idea that family is everything. You hear it ten thousand times a day. When you have the point of view that family is everything, all of your direction in life has to be filtered through their direction.

What Have You Decided Family Is?

What have you decided family is? Family might be your mom and your dad. Family might be your culture. Family might be your country.

Gary came to understand a more expansive definition of family when he got married to his second wife, who had a fifteen-year-old son. They were in the hot tub one night and Gary asked his stepson, "Well, how does it feel to have a real family?"

"What are you talking about?"

"You know, now you have a mom and a dad and extra brothers and sisters."

"I've always had a real family. My mom, my sister, and I are a real family."

Gary looked at that. "Oh. That's a pragmatic view. Who you have in your life is who your family is. Not who you're married to. Not who you're connected to and all that. You have to be willing to look at family from a different point of view."

And you have to see that family becomes a limitation in the places where it stultifies and limits your awareness.

Do You Have a Responsibility to Your Family?

Many people have asked us, "But isn't there a certain responsibility to your family?"

Responsibility means the ability to respond quickly and easily. It's not about you being in charge or in control. It's not that you are the reason or justification for anything. It's about *response*-ability. It's the recognition that you are not the reason anybody chooses anything.

Clearing: How Much of Your Awareness Are You Stultifying with the Family You Are Holding onto for Dear Life?

How much of your awareness are you stultifying with the family you are holding onto for dear life? Everything that is times a godzillion, will you destroy and uncreate it all? Right and Wrong, Good and Bad, All 9, POD and POC, Shorts Boys and Beyonds.

> Ask, "What energy, space, and consciousness can I be that will allow my child to grow up to be whoever he or she desires to be with total ease?"

12

WORKING WITH PEOPLE IN A PRAGMATIC WAY

When Susanna began to work in mental health in Sweden, she saw patients who had all kinds of issues. She had a lot of frustration about traditional psychology. She kept thinking, "This is not leading to what I know is truly possible. This is not the freedom that can come from awareness." When she discovered Access, she thought she had all the answers. Her attitude was, "I have these new tools now. I'm going change the world!"

But you can't go into a situation with answers before you've asked a question. You can't operate from theories or studies or beliefs that tell you how people are, how they are going to act, or why they respond the way they do. You have to be *in the question*. This is difficult about the whole field of psychology. There is not much question in it.

Fortunately, Susanna realized that her conclusions about what her clients needed were not going to change the world at all. They were just another stultification. So, she began to take a pragmatic approach and ask questions like,

- What can this person hear?
- What is he or she willing to receive?
- Is this person willing to change anything?

What Works Is Different for Each Person

You have to deal with people as they are. You do that by asking questions like, "What's going to work with this person?" What works is different for each person; no two people are exactly alike. When you ask questions, you develop an awareness of different directions things could take in the future. Most people don't do this. They go directly to conclusion, which takes them out of productivity and creation and places them in the middle of the stultification of this reality.

It doesn't matter whether people come to you for psychological counseling or a tarot reading. If this is what they want from you, this is what you give them — even if what you'd like to offer them is Access. Let people choose what they choose. That is allowance. It's their life; it's their choice.

This is something we have to learn with our kids. We must realize *it is their life*. They have to choose what works for them.

Change Comes from Allowance, Not from a Point of View

Susanna had many patients in mental health who *said* they wanted change. What people say, however, is not always what they choose. In her work, she always asks herself,

- Is this person interested in change?
- Will they choose it?

Choosing change is not better than not choosing change. There is no right or wrong or good or bad. People choose what they choose, and they can change their choice, especially when you gift them allowance. Invite people to change. Don't make them wrong for not changing what you have decided they should change.

In her training as a psychotherapist, Susanna was taught to have an objective, or a certain outcome, in mind with every patient. In practice, she realized this doesn't work. Having an objective forces you to have a point of view about an outcome, keeping you from being present and in allowance with what is. Change comes from allowance, not from a point of view.

Our purpose with Access is offering people the space to *choose*. When people begin to choose — and have total allowance for *what* they choose — they start to do what works for them.

How Can You Change Someone's Point of View?

People often tell us that they want to change somebody else's point of view. "How can I do that?" they ask.

When you don't align and agree with, or resist and react, to someone's point of view, that point of view begins to disintegrate out of their world and yours. You simply know what you know and put that into their space. You acknowledge, "I know this. This is what I am aware of." It is done without words and without force. You don't impose your point of view. You do it without speaking a word. And because people are psychic, they pick up what you say and assume it is their own point of view.

True Caring

Allowance is seen as a wrongness in both traditional psychology and this reality. You're not *supposed* to be in allowance of other people's stupidities, right? You are supposed to save them, change them, or control them. You're not supposed to allow them to be who they are. But is that true caring? Not at all.

True caring for others is the ability to give them only what they can have. You don't need to make them better, and you don't need to change them; you only need to care. Caring for others is recognizing that people know and that they will choose what they choose. They know what they are choosing even though they may say they don't.

And true caring for you is never buying somebody else's point of view. It's always knowing what is true for you.

What Seeds Are You Planting Right Now?

What seeds are you planting right now with what you're doing? You must acknowledge what you create in order to create more. Ask, "What am I creating here that I'm not acknowledging?"

A number of years ago, Susanna was scheduled to facilitate a small class in Tel Aviv, Israel. At the time, there were bombings going on in the city; there had been injuries and deaths. Susanna's parents were worried, and she was worried, too. Even though it didn't seem to make sense to travel a great distance to do a small class in such a dangerous environment, she knew she had to go.

It's now evident that the seeds she planted in Tel Aviv are blossoming into possibilities beyond this reality. We currently have over six hundred facilitators in Israel, including a facilitator in Tel Aviv who is working with Israeli soldiers and children who have PTSD, as well as an Israeli rabbi has approved the Access Bars.

The concept of quantum entanglements holds that all things are interrelated. Everything we do creates so much more than we acknowledge. Whatever is happening in this moment is having a quantum effect on everyone you've ever worked with and will ever work with, and all the people that they come in contact with in their lives. The effects of our actions ripple outward.

Moving Beyond the Conversation and Cognitizing of Mainstream Psychology

An Access facilitator once told us, "The more I work with clients, the more I find myself sitting in sessions with people feeling totally spaced out. Sometimes I don't even know what they just said."

We asked, "Are you actually spaced *out*? Or are you spaced *in* to possibilities?"

Most of us have the idea that we are spaced out if we are not focused. That's not necessarily so. The question is, what becomes possible beyond *cognitizing*? The tools we use in Access — the clearings and verbal processes as well as the Bars, all of which are hands-on processes — are about reaching what cannot be reached and changed by *cognitizing*.

This way of working with people is so beyond what is accepted in this reality. When Gary first began doing the Bars on people, it was hard for him to believe that he was having success of any kind. Then, one day, somebody walked in and told him, "You know how you did the Bars on me? After the first session, the pain I'd had in my feet for the last five years went away. I didn't tell you at the time because I was afraid it would come back, but it hasn't."

You *do not have to cognitize* what you are creating with a class, your business, a relationship, or anything else. You do not have to be able to define and explain what you're doing. You can simply ask, "Universe, show me what it is that I'm creating." This is where you plant seeds that can blossom beyond your control.

Working with people in a pragmatic way is about the joy of awareness of what you change in their universe. It's the celebration of what you are gifting them by the space you are. You have absolutely no point of view when you do this. You have no need for them to get it or not get it.

Information and Tools You Can Use in Working with Sensing and Feeling in Yourself and Others

Shortly after one of our events, a participant told us, "When I got home, I felt terrible. I had to cry and cry to dissipate all the energy from other people that got locked into my body."

A lot of people have this experience when they're in groups, but it doesn't have to be this way. We can *sense* things, or we can *feel* them. When you feel these things, you say, "I feel this person's pain," or "I feel what is going on with this person," and it gets locked into your body. *Feeling* things turns your body's capacity to perceive into a disability.

You need to know that pain is created by a person in their own body. You can *feel* people's pain, or you can *sense* what creates the pain. If you're used to feeling others' pain, it is not easy to change this. You have to train yourself because in this reality we are taught to *feel* everything. We rarely acknowledge the difference between what we *sense* and what we *feel*. *Sensing* allows us to have empathy without allowing others' pain to get locked into our bodies.

"I sense how much pain you have" is a whole different universe from feeling what someone feels. You have to get really clear in your own universe and be aware of what you sense in people.

Try this out. The next time you're in a room with other people, let your body feel the pain in somebody else's body. When you *feel* their pain or discomfort, you say, "I feel how badly your body feels," and your body increases the pain you feel. When you *sense* the pain or discomfort someone has within their body, you don't have to lock it into your body.

People Who Cut Themselves

An Access facilitator had experience working with people who cut themselves. She asked us, "What is that about?"

People who harm themselves in that way have no awareness of where they are in the scheme of things. They feel so much of other people's stuff and figure that if they cut themselves enough they will feel their own body. This is often the case with any kind of masochism.

People are trying to feel their own body, to feel themselves.

The facilitator asked, "How can I help clients who are doing that?"

We suggested asking them questions and talking about the difference between sensing and feeling. First, ask them, "What is the value of cutting yourself? What do you love about cutting yourself?" They may say they feel more alive or less numb. You can also say, "Let's leave *feeling* alone for a minute. You can *sense* your body, right? Does your body love what you are doing to it?"

When you give your clients this information about sensing and feeling and the difference between them, you empower them to know what they know. They may start to realize something different: "Oh, I have a different choice here. I had no idea. I thought my only choice was to cut myself because when I do that, I can feel myself. I realize now that, instead of feeling, I can use my sensing and not allow the pain to get locked in."

Sadness Is a Choice

It's the same with other people's sadness. When you are hyper aware of the sadness that everybody lives with, you accept that sadness as a fact in your universe. You tend to say, "Everybody's sad. This is a fact." But sadness is not a fact. It's a choice people make.

We assume people are choice-less—rather than recognizing that their sadness is something they're choosing.

Some people intentionally wear shoes that hurt. Why? Maybe because they want to be stylish. No matter how painful the shoes are, they wear them non-stop, all day long. Why would they choose that? People do the same thing with sadness. They choose their pain; they choose their sadness.

What is the value of choosing sadness? Well, for one thing, it enables people to avoid anger. People on this planet think they have only two choices: sadness or anger. They don't realize that happiness is also a choice. Joy is not on their radar because they didn't grow up with people who had joy.

You have to acknowledge that people choose to be sad, and that there are places in the world where people don't choose sadness. When Gary was a kid, he loved going to parties hosted by his Hispanic and Dutch friends. Everyone would be dancing. Little kids and old ladies would be dancing as much as everyone else. The young guys would ask the old ladies to dance. Everyone was included in the joy.

There are incredible examples of people choosing happiness. We were sent a YouTube video about a six-year-old boy who lost his mother in an accident and his father to cancer. This boy looked at all the sadness around him and he said, "You know what? I am going to start smiling." He got that smiling was a choice. He started smiling at everybody, everybody smiled back, and it became infectious. He wasn't going to let sadness rule his life. He said, "My life is going to be different. I am not going to live for sadness. I am going to live for joy."

Some people don't want to incorporate joy into their lives because they think that if they are joyful it will exacerbate the sadness of others. That isn't so. Those sad, unhappy people can't even imagine what you're doing. They assume that if you're happy, you must be on some kind of drug.

There Is No Need to Protect Yourself from Anything

Many of us try to stay away from people who are sad or in pain because we don't want to feel what they're feeling. That's one reason people have gated communities. They want to stay away from sadness and keep in the people who are as mundane as they are.

Contrary to what you may think, there is no need to protect yourself from anything. In fact, when you try to protect yourself, you exclude everything, including information that could be vital to you. Is that what you really want to do? Plus, it takes a lot of energy to put up walls and barriers. It's much easier to practice receiving everything.

When Susanna was studying psychotherapy, she and her classmates were trained to protect themselves from their patients by creating barriers and using coping strategies. She immediately got that this was not the way she wanted to be with people. She didn't want to be distracted from being with her patients; she wanted to be present with them.

Being a trickster, she asked the teacher, "Are our patients dangerous?" One of the strategies being taught was to imagine a river between herself and the patient. It was clear to her that this was a major distraction from being present with the person she was working with. So, in her mischievous way, she asked the teacher, "Are there fish in the river? Are there flowers on the riverbank?"

When Susanna graduated and started to work with clients as a psychologist, she saw how exhausting it was to try to protect herself from people rather than simply receiving everything the person in front of her was saying. It was much easier to simply *be* with people—with all their sadness and troubles. She says, "When you don't put up barriers around you, you gain so much more information about a person. It's like opening a treasure chest full of information waiting to be used. Awareness is not a curse; it is the gift that keeps on gifting. All it takes is for you to be willing to receive."

Panic Attacks

Let's say a friend of yours is having a panic attack. His heart is racing; he feels weak, dizzy, and out of control. Ask calmly and firmly, "Who does this belong to?" He may start getting calm immediately as he realizes that none of the things he is feeling are his in the first place.

Panic is not a *sickness;* it is an *awareness.* By asking, "Who does this belong to?" you acknowledge what is true for the person. Acknowledgment of what is true for somebody, by itself, creates relaxation.

Sometimes with panic attacks, people have checked out to an extreme extent. In those situations, it may be necessary for you to be sharp and intense in your energy and say, "No. You are present here, right now, with me."

People often ask us what they can do to help clients or friends who have panic attacks. We say, "Please don't buy into the reality of panic attacks. Don't go, 'Oh, poor you.' Don't let people control or manipulate you by having a panic attack. Instead, be the energy that invites them to be present. Use the tool of asking, 'Who does this belong to?'"

When somebody has a panic attack, it's easy to get swept away. You might find yourself getting stressed and trying to do something to handle the situation. This often worsens the situation, as you validate the person's panic attack as a foregone reality.

When someone is having a panic attack, try to be as calm as possible. Ask yourself, "What do I know here? What space and ease can I be to change this with total ease?" By being ease and space, you show the person what is possible. You do not buy into their panic and, with that, make it even more real.

Tears and Hysteria

Tears are a natural part of sadness, but they can also be a way of avoiding being present. Sometimes they are a way of rejecting what is being said to you. Once somebody stops crying, they stop creating drama and start creating awareness. When they begin to do that, things start working for them.

For example, Gary received a call once from a lady who was crying hysterically. He said, "Stop crying! I can't understand a word you're saying." She did. Then he asked her, "Is any of this real, or are you creating it? Who does this belong to?"

It turned out that she had been watching a documentary about Angola Prison, the largest maximum security prison in America. Gary's questions enabled her to see that she had been channeling the pain of every single prisoner.

Phobias

You can also use the question "Who does this belong to?" with people who have phobias. An Access facilitator told us that a client of hers had a phobia about needles. The client couldn't have blood drawn, and she started to faint in health class when they talked about abortions. It progressed to being unable to drive on the freeway if there was construction.

We told her to use the tool of asking her client, "Who does this belong to?" We also suggested these questions:

- What do you get from having phobias?
- What is the benefit of your phobia?
- How do you win with your phobia?
- How do others lose from your phobia?

Phobias are often about winning and losing, and people use them as a way of winning over others. You can control people with your phobias. A phobia is a losing position for the other person, while the person with the phobia sees himself or herself as the winner.

The facilitator acknowledged that her client was likely doing that. Perhaps this client didn't truly want to get well. In fact, she won every time she had a phobia. Her mindset was, "I have a phobia, therefore I can't…." or "Therefore you have to…." It was about having everyone else adjust to her reality.

One of the patients Susanna worked with had several different phobias and frequent panic attacks. His whole family would tiptoe around him to make sure he did not have another attack and that everything was under control.

Susanna asked him, "What do you love about your phobias? What is the value of them for you?"

His reply was incredibly honest and telling: "When I have a panic attack, I have my whole world wrapped around my little finger."

Is that wrong? No, it is what it is. When you see things for what they are, you have choice.

Allergies

Sometimes people try to control the environment with their allergies. You can ask them,

- What do you win by having an allergy?
- What do you lose by having an allergy?

They say, "I can't be here with that ____!"

You say, "Okay, you can't be here. Do you win with that or do you lose with that?"

If they're being honest, they'll say, "I win!"

Then you can ask, "Really? How many people don't want to be with you because you win?"

All of these things — allergies, phobias, hysteria, panic attacks — are about who is winning and who is losing. It is a *win-lose* universe for these people. They are more interested in winning than they are in changing.

Once they begin to tell you what is true for them about winning and losing, all of a sudden they will say, "Wait a minute! This isn't working." At this point they can choose something different.

Anxiety

People buy anxiety from others in order to prove they are like them. Anything that comes up for you — whether it's sadness, anger, anxiety, depression, or any other kind of craziness — is an interpretation of what *is* that actually *isn't*. Anxiety is a creation. It is an invention and not a reality. It can only exist when you cut off your awareness and give anxiety a role in the theatre you call your life. Try asking,

- What invention are you using to create the anxiety you are choosing?
- And whose is it?

Generosity of Spirit vs. Envy and Jealousy

Consider some common judgments of women who are beautiful and rich: "I hate the fact that she has what she's got. I hate the fact that she looks the way she looks. I hate the fact, I hate fact, I hate the fact…."

You have to get rid of "facts" as a reality because nothing is a fact except when you make it so.

People make their facts real in order to justify why they can't receive something the other person has to offer. This is just another way people cut off their receiving. Every fact is designed to cut off receiving and cut off greater awareness.

A woman told us about feeling envy while watching her young cousin riding a horse: "She is young and skinny and beautiful. I looked at her and I got the awareness of how people respond when they see someone who looks like they are perfect and rich and happy."

Of course, they're not perfect. It's an image. It fits a picture that other people can't have, so they reject it. They think, "I want that but I can't have it." "I want" means "I lack of it," which means "I can't have it," which means "I will never choose that," which means they have to be envious.

People who can't receive are envious; they're not jealous. *Envy* means you want what somebody else has. *Jealousy* means you try to hold onto what you have for fear that someone is going to take it from you.

People are envious of others who have what they don't have. It's as though they think that if they can take something away from the other person, it will be theirs. But since they have already decided they can't have it, guess what? They can't have it! So they reject it.

You can see something you like and simply be aware that you like it; you can reject it or try to destroy it; or you can ask,

- What do I have to change in order to have that?
- Where do I have to go?
- Who do I have to talk to?

You can go into question. You can be happy that the other person has what they have and say, "How cool they have that! I would like that, too. What is possible for me to get that with ease?" That is generosity of spirit.

You don't look at your friend's great dress and say, "*She* shouldn't have that! *I* should have gotten it." Instead you say, "Look what she got! It's beautiful!" Generosity of spirit comes from being willing to question how you can add to your life — not how you can get something from somebody else. You are happy when people have more, and you are happy to receive more yourself. Whenever you have a moment where you say, "It's not okay that this person has that," ask,

- Who does this belong to?
- What have I made a fact that is not a fact?

In asking these questions, you're creating the future you would like to have.

*Caring for others is recognizing that people know,
and that they will choose what they choose.*

*They know what they are choosing,
even though they may say they don't.*

*And true caring for you is never buying
somebody else's point of view.*

It's always knowing what is true for you.

13

MARKETING YOURSELF: CREATING THE PACKAGE

Gary had a very pragmatic teacher who was born in England in 1913. Mary believed in metaphysics. She traveled all over the world to every metaphysical class, group, and psychic teacher known to mankind. Her husband had a completely different outlook. Bill believed you lived once and then moldered in the ground. These differences didn't stop them from having an extraordinary relationship based on honor, trust, allowance, vulnerability, and gratitude for one another.

In the 1950s, Bill was working as an advertising executive in New York. "Mary," he would say, "I need you to go out to dinner with me to meet my clients, but please do not talk about any of that weird stuff you do." Mary would put on a nice conservative dress and her jewels, and she would present the image of a charming, conventional wife. She never presented what she knew; she just got interested in everybody she met and asked them questions. Most everyone, Bill's clients included, thought she was incredibly intelligent and remarkable.

Be Interested in Everyone

Mary was a genius at marketing herself. People loved to talk with her, and she always had an abundance of clients with whom she shared her metaphysical work. Her secret was being interested in everyone. She knew that all you need to do to look like the most intelligent and knowledgeable person in the world is stop talking about yourself and get interested in everybody else. Ask people about themselves. Ask and shut up. Never tell anything about you, and they will find you the most fascinating individual they ever met.

It's like when you go on a first date. If you're smart, you don't talk. You ask questions. You show that you are interested in the other person. Most people want to be *interesting* rather than *interested*, but that won't get you what you want. You have to learn to be *interested*. If you are interested, people will always ask for more of what you have to give. This is true marketing: Be available and interested.

We suggested this to a woman who said, "Yeah, but people say such stupid things. I'm not interested in talking to them."

Conclusions like that shut down possibilities. She had concluded, "I can't be bothered with this person. I have no interest in him or her." Every conclusion you reach creates a place where you do not allow people to contribute who might contribute to you. Instead of coming to a conclusion, ask some questions:

- What can this person do?
- What can he be?
- How can she contribute to my life and my reality?

Susanna's dream is that psychology and psychotherapy will become more interested in the patient, rather than focusing on theories about what's wrong with them. Clients know so much. You can be the facilitator who makes it easier for them to know what they know. How do you do this? By being interested, by not having a point of view or an objective, and by asking questions. Try it — and watch how much people's lives expand, including yours.

Choose Elegance

To market yourself, you have to present yourself in a way that people will respond to. This means dressing well. When you present yourself in a way that is attractive to people, you make a great impression. People will think, "He is so well turned out," or "She dresses so beautifully."

You have to start choosing elegance. Whether it's a pant suit or a short skirt or slacks and a shirt, choose elegance. This is especially true if you're young because people tend to dismiss young professionals based on their age. If you are young and elegant, you are brilliant and timeless.

A lady came to Access and asked Gary to be her mentor. At the time, her hair was dyed three different colors. He told her, "Look, you have to dress differently if you want to be successful in business. You are twenty-five and unless you dress in something classy and timeless, people are going to dismiss you."

At first she said, "I won't do that. This is who I am." But she wasn't getting any clients, so she took Gary's advice and changed the way she dressed for one class. She got three new clients. After that, she returned to her old way of dressing, and those clients went away.

You have to make the package look the way people want it to look. Be pragmatic. Who has the money to pay you for the services you offer? Young people or old people? Most likely it's old people. So if you're young, you have to appear timeless. You can put on a Chanel dress or Chanel pants and people will say, "Oh! That is Chanel." People who have money know these things.

Sometimes people hear this and say, "Okay, but I don't want to dress like an old person." You don't have to dress like an old person! We're suggesting that you dress with style and class. Go shopping with someone who can help you pick great, classy stuff. Choose someone who functions in the world in which class exists.

Some people have an innate sense of class and elegance. Gary and one of his daughters were at a garage sale when she was eight years old.

"Dad, I want this wallet," she said.

"Why, honey?" he asked.

"Because it's DKNY."

She was eight years old. She is now a woman who dresses in a timeless and classic style.

His other daughter loved hippie clothes and dressed that way for a long time. One day Gary had a talk with her: "You have got to dress better, darling. You have to step up your style." She changed the way she dressed and more people started saying, "Tell me about what you do."

People will get interested in you when you create the package to look the right way. They will instantly assume you have information they want, and they will listen to what you have to say. This is called the pragmatics of awareness. You are aware that people have points of view and you ask, "How do I use their points of view to create what I want?"

Ask: How Can I Use This Package to My Advantage?

You are unique to a degree that you don't yet acknowledge. You don't see how unique you are; you don't appreciate the value of that. The value of your uniqueness has nothing to do with your physical attributes, however wonderful, beautiful, and sexy they may be. Those are simply additional assets. They are the packaging you have available. You have to look at those things and say, "Okay. This is the package. How can I use the package to my advantage?"

Go to Social Events

If you're in business, you need to go to social events. Are they fun? No. Are they annoying? Yes. Is there anybody there you want to talk to? Usually not. You just have to stand there quietly with your glass of champagne and somebody will come up to you and ask, "Who are you and what do you do?" That one person could bring twenty people into your business.

We have a very elegant and pragmatic friend who is great at marketing herself and always has an abundance of clients in her business. Whenever she notices that she could use a few new clients to fill in her calendar, she says, "Time to go to a cocktail party!"

*People will get interested in you when you
create the package to look the right way.
They will instantly assume you have information they want,
and they will listen to what you have to say.
This is called the pragmatics of awareness.*

14

THE POINT WHERE ALL THINGS BECOME POSSIBLE

A man asked Gary, "How do I get more awareness?"

Gary said, "By relaxing."

"But that means I have to do nothing."

"Where did you get the point of view that relaxation is doing nothing?" Gary asked. "I relax with everything I choose and everything I do."

Awareness is the ultimate source of total relaxation because you never have to question anything when you know. You never have to doubt yourself when you know. You never have to ask whether you are choosing right or wrong when you know. Full awareness and full knowing come with total relaxation.

When you actually know something, you can relax because you don't have to fight. Let's say you know that your partner is going to yell at you for not doing what he or she wants you to do. You can relax and just listen to what your partner has to say.

Relaxation and knowing come with a level of allowance. You are willing to be the space that other people cannot assault. How different is that from "No! I have to avoid this! What do I have to change to make sure he doesn't yell? How can I take away the need in her world to yell?"

Change in this reality is all about overcoming something rather than relaxing into the change that is available. Most of us tend to use force when we decide we are going to change something. We say, "This is horrible! I have to change this. How could I be so stupid again?"

What if you could relax with everything you choose and everything you do?

Clearing: What Have You Made So Vital About Never Being Totally Relaxed?

What have you made so vital about never being totally relaxed that creates the need, necessity, and desire of limited awareness in order to create the necessity of being uptight and unaware? Everything that is, will you destroy and uncreate it all? Right and Wrong, Good and Bad, All 9, POD and POC, Shorts, Boys, and Beyonds.

If you really want to create possibility in your life, you have to be willing to relax and have awareness of everything. Otherwise, all you're doing is choosing from the limited menu of somebody else's reality. What would happen if you asked, "What can I be or do differently to listen to my awareness totally?"

Are You Avoiding the Complexity and the Joy of Creating Possibility?

Most people tend to create just enough complacency and comfort in their lives to feel vaguely content and satisfied. They are creating some comfort, but they are avoiding the challenge of possibility.

- Are you avoiding the complexity and the joy of creating possibility?
- If you were willing to choose beyond what you have currently chosen, what would be possible for you that is not possible for others?

Becoming a Being Who Can Create Worlds and Possibilities

What would happen if you were willing to acknowledge that you are an omnipotent being? Webster's Dictionary 1828 defines *omnipotent* as, "Almighty; possessing unlimited power; all powerful." Then it offers, as an example, this sentence: "The being that can create worlds must be omnipotent."

This is what we are asking you to be: A being who can create possibilities, even worlds. Many people do not want to be omnipotent. Why? Because it means you have no justifications for the limitations you call your life.

We understand why people don't want to be omnipotent. In this reality, you are not supposed to be that potent. This reality is about fitting in and being normal.

We have seen time after time that people can *choose* a level of ease and joy that goes far beyond what their family and friends and colleagues could ever choose. But once they notice how powerful their joy has made them, they sometimes go back to sadness to engage the familiarity of limitation again. Joy and ease make you powerful. Joy and ease are also intimidating.

- How powerful are you allowing yourself to be?
- How unscathed by the limitations of this reality are you allowing yourself to be?
- How willing are you to allow yourself to soar above what others make real?

Clearing: Receiving the Title *Omnipotent Infinite Being*

What energy, space, and consciousness are you refusing to perceive, know, be, and receive about the title of *Omnipotent Infinite Being* that would allow you to change the world with total ease? Everything that doesn't allow that to show up, will you destroy and uncreate it all? Right and Wrong, Good and Bad, All 9, POD and POC, Shorts, Boys, and Beyonds.

You Don't Have to Fight Against This Reality to Create a New Reality

Access facilitators often have the idea that creating an Access class requires force and effort. People also have this idea about their businesses, their families, their relationships. They have a target for what they want to create, and they think that force and effort are required to create a result. But you don't have to fight against this reality in order to create a new reality.

When Gary gives a class, for example, he looks at what he can do to invite people to be more than they have ever been willing to be. It's an invitation, not a target. That's an important difference. There is no force or control involved in what he does. It's about ease and making a contribution to someone else's capacities. It's the gentleness of a different reality.

Can you receive the gentleness of all possibility? Or do you resist the gentleness of things in favor of getting hit with a two-by-four upside your head? Are you thinking that getting smacked by a piece of wood is what's needed to make you change? Is that the intensity you need in order to know that you are really choosing? The two-by-four hits you in the head, and you say, "I have no choice. I have to change!"

Every problem can be turned into a possibility when you allow all of life to come to you with ease and joy and glory.

Creating from the Exquisite Moments of Being

If you didn't have to fight this reality, what would you be creating from? You'd be creating from the exquisite moments of being. You'd be creating from the exquisite choices of being. If we would all choose the exquisite moments and choices of being, a different world would show up for us.

You have hopes and dreams that you call desires, and you tend to think that if you desire something…it will actualize. But does it occur in that way? It doesn't. That's because desire has nothing to do with actualization.

What Comes to You Is the Result of the Choices You Make

What comes to fruition for you is not the result of desire. What comes to you is a result of the choices you make. When you are willing to make choices and do what works — when you are willing to be pragmatic about the choices that *will* work — everything you desire will come to fruition.

The more people we can get to have the awareness of what they are capable of, the more possibilities we can get to show up in the world. That's what's important.

Most of us tend to look at what we need or what we want our body to do or be rather than choosing what would create a gentle ease for all eternity. We try to force things into existence. We fight for whatever we've decided to create. But that's not the way things work.

The space of change is like snow falling on a winter day. There is no force in it.

Think about New York City when it snows. It is quiet. Is New York City ever quiet? Yes, when it snows and everything becomes still. You have to get to the place where everything is like newly fallen snow, where there is a sense of peace in your entire world. There is no necessity, no angst, and no need. That's when all things become possible.

The Gentleness of All Possibility

Most people don't have any idea what gentleness is. Look at flowers. You might say, "Flowers are gentle." But are you sure? Go look at some. Are they gentle or are they vibrant? Or are they both? They are gentle, *and* there is a vibrancy about them. When you become as gentle as you actually are, there is a vibrancy about you that invites everybody into your reality. It's the gentleness of possibility. The greatest gift you are is the gentleness of possibility. It's the greatest choice you make.

You may find that there's an intensity present when you are being the gentleness of possibilities, but it doesn't come from force or solidity. It comes from total space. Possibilities are always about space.

This reality's point of view about creation is that you have to be out there, people have to see you, and you have to have intensity in order to be seen and heard. In this reality, everything is about conclusion, results, completion, need, and desire. People think this is the way it's got to be. This is not so. When you are willing to be the infinite space of infinite possibilities, everything is gentle and easy. Effort ceases.

What energy, space, and consciousness can you be to become the gentleness of infinite possibilities for all eternity?

15

QUESTIONS AND TOOLS YOU CAN USE TO OPEN THE DOORS OF POSSIBILTY

A question always empowers. That's because when you ask a question, the universe does its best to help you out. An answer disempowers. Answers, conclusions, and judgments fill the space. Questions create space, and when you create space you open the door for more possibilities to show up. The choice for space creates possibility, and the universe has your back when you are embracing and celebrating space.

A question is always the key to opening the doors of possibility. You'll never see those doors, you'll never know where they are, let alone be able to open them, if you don't ask a question. It's always the pragmatic thing to do.

Getting serious does not open the doors to possibility. Asking questions does. What have you made so vital about the seriousness of life that keeps you from the joy and the ease of living?

Here are some more Access questions and tools you can use to open the doors of possibility:

Tool: What Else Is Possible?

Do you often say, "That's impossible"?

What might be possible if you didn't say, "That's impossible"?

One of the best tools for discovering what's possible is asking, "What else is possible?" A lady we know used this question when she went up to an airline counter with her baggage. The guy at the counter put her bag on the scale and said, "Your baggage is twenty pounds overweight. I'm going to have to charge you for this."

The lady smiled and asked, "What else is possible?"

The guy was confused and went to talk with his supervisor. The supervisor walked over to the lady and said, "I'm sorry, but your baggage is twenty pounds overweight. We have to charge you for it."

Again, the lady smiled and asked, "What else is possible?"

The supervisor stood there for a moment. He looked at the lady and looked at the bag. Then, with a big smile, he turned around, tagged her bag, and sent it through.

What else is possible is a multi-use question that allows you to be aware of possibilities you cannot see when you have a point of view about something. Use it when something shows up in your life that you appreciate and when something shows up that you do not appreciate. Use it when you catch yourself in a judgment. Use it when you don't know what to do. Use it when you wish to open the door to a new possibility.

Instead of Judging, Use "What Else Is Possible?"

Because Access is an international business, we go to lots of different countries and we take lots of different currencies. If we accept a currency in one country, we have to pay 4-6 percent to get it converted into US currency. We are trying to find a bank that will carry our cash separately in Euros, US dollars, and Aussie dollars until we need to use them, but no bank will do that. They take the money we earn in their country and convert it to US dollars, and then when we want to pay a bill in their currency, they charge us another 4-6 percent to convert it back into their currency.

It doesn't seem fair, but it's just the cost of doing business. If we judge them as bad banks, we shut the door on other possibilities. But if we ask, "What else is possible?" we open the door to possibilities.

When someone gets a psychological diagnosis, instead of resisting and reacting, they can ask, "What else is possible?" Maybe they will discover that the diagnosis is an award for their difference and excellence!

Tool: What Else Is Possible with Part of My Work?

When Susanna was working in mental health, she had to do neuropsychological tests on patients. After a while conducting the same tests over and over again, she started to get bored and resent her work. She asked, "What else is possible with this part of my work that I have not yet considered?"

Right after she asked that question, she discovered a way to use the tests to strengthen people's knowing. She would show them the difference between knowing and thinking by asking, "What do you *know* is the right answer here? And what do you *think* is the right answer?" The patients discovered that knowing is instantaneous and thinking takes longer and requires calculating and concluding—and it is less correct than knowing. All that from one question: "What else is possible?"

Tool: How Does It Get Any Better Than This?

When you have a situation that is not working well for you, do you define it as difficult or a disaster? What does that do energetically? It solidifies the situation as a problem and perpetuates the wrongness. What if you asked, "How does it get any better than this?"

Susanna was once at an Advanced Body class that Gary was facilitating. Some people were sitting next to her while she was getting a body process run, and they were pretty noisy. She didn't go to conclusion, judgment, or answer. She didn't even have any point of view about the noise they were creating. She didn't try to force the noisy people out or push them away energetically. She simply asked, "How does it get any better than this? What else is possible here?" Suddenly one of them said, "I can't hear Gary very well from here. Let's move somewhere else."

We often try to figure out *how* something is going to get better. But it is not really about figuring out the *how*. It is about asking the question, "How does it get any better than this?" which invites the ease you think you cannot have.

Whenever you are in a stuck situation, ask, "How does it get any better than this?" Be willing to ask it as often it takes. When Susanna is working with patients, she asks this question regularly. Sometimes, in the middle of a session that seemed almost hopeless, either Susanna or the client will say something that brings light to the matter.

Tool: Indulge the Thought

An attractive woman once came to an Access class that Dr. Dain Heer and Gary were teaching. Dain thought she was beautiful and wonderful; he couldn't stop talking about her. Gary said, "I think you should indulge the thought of taking on this woman and her two children." He got Dain to indulge the idea of living with her and her kids and what that would be like. After doing this for three days, Dain said, "You know what? I am not that interested in her anymore."

Try it. Indulge what you think you would like and what you think you can't have and see what your life would be like if you chose it.

Use this tool when you meet someone you think you want to live with. Indulge the thought of what it would be like to be married to this person's entire family. Look at each individual in the family. Once you begin to indulge the thought, chances are you will be running the other way as fast as your little legs can take you.

Trying to figure out beforehand what you should do is a shortcut to driving you crazy. Have you ever done those pro and con lists? Was that fun for you? Indulging the thought is a much easier way. Rather than trying to get it right, indulge in what each choice will create as your future. In a short period of time, it becomes very obvious what works for you and what does not.

Tool: Acknowledge What Is

Gary was once driving a rental car in Scotland. From his point of view, as someone who drives in the United States, he was on the wrong side of the road. When he got to a roundabout, his brain froze. He couldn't figure out where he was supposed to go or what side of the street he was supposed to be on. He said, "I hate Scotland!" and suddenly his brain started to function again.

That's the power in acknowledging what is. When you feel like killing someone, just acknowledge that you want to kill them. Say, "I would love to kill this ____!" Suddenly you are over it. It's amazing how much better you feel. Your body relaxes. Your attitude changes.

Most parents don't love their children in every single moment of the day, and they tend to think this is horrible. But what if you acknowledge what is true for you in every moment? It is just a moment. Susanna was working with a mother who admitted that she had moments where she wished she did not have children. This was a difficult thing for her admit. She had suppressed so much anger that nearly every encounter with her kids was a ticking time bomb waiting to go off at any second. The day she simply acknowledged what was true for her, that she sometimes wished she didn't have kids, her relationship with her children changed and she could see how much she appreciated them.

Tool: What Would I Have to Be or Do Differently That Would Create a Different Possibility Here?

A class participant once told us, "I noticed recently that when I talk to people what people hear is completely different from what I say."

"It's always been that way," Gary replied. "You just never noticed it before. If you think people get what you say when you talk, you are insane. People don't hear what you are saying. They hear what they want to hear."

The woman said, "Yes, but all my life I've been very particular about using words that mean exactly what I want to say because I want people to understand me. I always try to be clear and concise when I talk to people."

Gary asked her, "Why would you talk *to* people instead of *with* people? I don't talk to people, I talk with them. We're in a class, and I'm talking *with* you, right? I'm following what you hear the way you hear it. I'm not following what I want you to hear from me. You're not acknowledging the awareness that what you are saying to people is being interpreted by them."

The joy of awareness is when you realize, *Oh, what I am saying is being interpreted by this person in this way.* You can celebrate the joy of awareness that what you say is being interpreted.

Then you ask,

- How can I use this to my advantage?
- What is possible with this?
- What would I have to be or do differently that would create a different possibility here?

Maybe you need to tell them a story. Maybe you have to be silent. Silence is a great technique to use, because when you're silent, people think they have to fill the space. They have the point of view that silence is a space you fill, not something you enjoy. So, when you are quiet, they fill the space and you get information about what is true for them. You get information about what they are *not* hearing because it will literally spill out of their mouth.

And what if you didn't have the point of view that people had to hear you? What if you already knew they were *not* hearing you? What if you had the point of view that *you* had to hear what *they* heard? What if you were only interested in what they were hearing?

When you're working with people and they're not hearing you, ask, "What would I have to be or do differently that would create a different possibility here?" Be aware that people can only hear what matches their points of view and judgments. It's not about what you would like them to hear but what they *choose* to hear. And it's about allowance.

Tool: What Awareness Can I Have Here That Would Erase All of This?

There are people who think that asking a question is about looking at something and saying, "Oh, that's where I've done that," and then letting it go. They're saying, "I'll take this one step."

That's nice, but what about asking, "What awareness can I have here that would erase all of this?" That question is about the light of awareness. It's a short cut. You've just opened the door. You now have a choice. What do you want to choose? We're not pushing you. We're inviting you to make a choice.

Pushing people to change *does not work at all*. If you want people to change, they will stick their feet in the mud, stay exactly where they are, and not change a single thing. But if you tell them, "Nah, don't change. It's fine. You're great the way you are," they will say, "No, I'm changing!" That's the way humanoids are.

Would you like to take this strategy a step further and have a little fun? When people tell you all about their problems, say, "That sounds horrible! Poor you! How can you manage with all this?" They will immediately tell you, "Oh, it's not really that bad." You just manipulated them out of their limitation by encouraging them to be more aware. Easy! The question erases the other person's insanity and your reaction to it.

Tool: What's Relevant Here?

Here's a tool you can use when you're receiving too much information. Let's say you want to install a new counter in your bathroom. You go online and search "bathroom counters." You get way too much information. What would happen if you did something with every link in front of you? You would go crazy.

The same thing happens with awareness. You might say, "I would like to know more about this and this and this," and suddenly there is so much information available to you. Imagine making it all relevant. Imagine saying, "I have to do something with all of this!"

When you are aware and receiving everything, you will have a lot of information coming at you. Some of the information will be relevant, and some won't be. You have to choose what is relevant for you.

When you are in a room full of people and there is whispering in the back of the room and ten thousand things are happening simultaneously, ask, "What part of this is relevant to my life?" and you'll hear what you need to hear. Some people try to filter information, but you don't need to do that. Nor do you need to categorize things. Just ask,

- What is relevant here?
- What is the one relevant thing in this that I could deal with?
- What part of this is relevant to my life?

The psychological point of view is that you must have selective hearing to be able to choose, but if you use these questions and are willing to be aware, your awareness will automatically select the information you desire. It's not about focusing. The most important thing will suddenly stand out and you will know that the rest is irrelevant. There is absolutely no effort or work to it. It is just, "There it is! Next!" You receive the information you need. You don't even know where it came from or how it got there.

Susanna was once on a date with a guy who knew a lot about politics. "He was really smart. I've never studied politics, and I had the point of view that I was stupid about that subject. Suddenly I recognized what I was doing and I thought, 'Oh! Interesting point of view.' Then I asked myself, 'So what do I know about politics?' I opened my mouth and all kinds of smart stuff came out, just like that. If you ask for what is relevant, what is relevant will become obvious to you. That's knowing. No work is required."

When you ask for what is relevant in your life, you will have an awareness of a future that you didn't even know could exist. When you ask for what is relevant, you will get that information, even though you don't need it now. You will receive information, in every single moment of every single day, about what is relevant for now and for the future — if you are willing to have that intensity of awareness.

Never Give Up, Never Give In, Never Quit

Pragmatic Psychology is about never giving up, never giving in, and never quitting, no matter what anybody says or does. You have to have the willingness to be here and know that you know. Do you realize how amazing you are that you are willing to know that you know?

- What leader are you that you haven't acknowledged you are?
- What are you capable of that other people can't even imagine?

*You have to function from the fact that
you always have a choice.
"I have a choice," you say.
"What would I like to choose?"
If you realize you always have a choice,
you can choose anything.*

CPSIA information can be obtained
at www.ICGtesting.com
Printed in the USA
LVHW040344261120
672724LV00029B/174